Mildred Downs Moore — 1928

A Unique Life

An Autobiography, Complete with Misdeeds

by

Mildred D. Rust, M.D.

DORRANCE PUBLISHING CO., INC.
PITTSBURGH, PENNSYLVANIA 15222

ISBN # 0-8059-6724-9
Printed in the United States of America

First Printing

For information or to order additional books, please write:
Dorrance Publishing Co., Inc.
701 Smithfield Street
Third Floor
Pittsburgh, Pennsylvania 15222
1-800-788-7654
or visit our web site and on-line catalog at www.dorrancepublishing.com

Dedicated to the memory of
my most significant significant other,
Lou,

and to my co-struggler,
Frances, my dear sister.

CONTENTS

FOREWORD

MILLIE, AS HER FRIENDS CALL HER, HAS SET DOWN AN ACCOUNT OF HER FIRST SEVENTY-five years that shines with honesty, love, and courage. The story takes us from her earliest beginnings to the most recent dramatic turns in her journey, giving us the chance to get to know her beloved father and sister as well as her treasured children, friends, and colleagues and how they all helped her to develop into the wise and thoughtful person who emerges in these pages. Millie stimulates us to reflect on our own lives and the dramas and ironies they contain.

"I am human and nothing human is alien to me" could be the motto of this account as the challenges, physical and psychological, that Millie accepts—sometimes without choice but often by design—unfold. She shows us the hand she was dealt and how she played it, making special reference (as indicated by the subtitle) to her mistakes of commission and omission and the aftermath of guilt and sadness they left in their wake. The themes of her life as helper of troubled psychiatric patients, devoted mother, faithful friend, caretaker of pets, and music lover all can be traced to what she experienced in the early years in that big house in New Jersey that is carefully described and then visualized through clever diagrams. (This is an example of Millie's attention to the small details that keep us attached to the reality of the stage on which her story is played out.)

It seems that the nuclear family's heart was always open to others in need of shelter or support and service and sharing of what was available was an everyday occurrence as Millie and her younger sister took their places at the table. There were grandparents and maiden aunts as well as cousins in the cluster. And there was both financial success and hard times as the background at different times. It seems that nothing ever came easy for Millie and her family. From the beginning of her days there was a deformity of her feet to contend with, necessitating much medical intervention and leaving her with lifelong compensations to make. The complications involved a deeply ambivalent connection with her mother whose physical attention to her feet exceeded, by a long time, Millie's comfort with it. And there was a social inhibition which from time to time overwhelmed her as she fought to find her place among her peers.

The earliest of a long series of losses began with grandparents, as it does for many people. As she reports each of these, Millie notes her reactions. Many times, she tells us simply, "I didn't grieve." The ability to report her deep feelings with honesty and clarity—be they fear, shame, guilt, rage, or (frequently) sadness—calls on the reader to face one's own unpleasant affects with equal honesty. The frequent references to psychotherapy and the therapists who have worked with her suggest an origin for some of this courageous self-analysis and disclosure.

The organization of this book is one in which both the chronological and the thematic approaches have been utilized so a kind of Gestalt emerges as the pieces fit together with some acceptable overlap. We learn that Millie's family of origin supports her intellectual growth and the reward is being a valedictorian. There is a love of good music in the house and Millie develops lifelong joy in choral singing that also becomes the basis of a part of her social competence. The family's capacity to adapt to reversals due to change in the economic climate and tough out the tough times builds in her a strength to cope with reversals. Some of them are heart breaking as, for example, the discovery at three months of age of her first child's severe uncorrectable birth defect. There is also the continuation of the succession of losses and the eventual breakup of her marriage. Through these and many other difficult times, Millie perseveres and emulates how one can turn to others for help, accept one's mistakes and weaknesses, and still look forward with hope.

What sustained her comes through clearly. Millie draws on her Unitarian Universalist faith, her continuing participation in making music, her friendships, professional support, and the love of her family members.

All these and her refusal to give in to despair led Millie to her happiest time—a loving, sustaining relationship that lasted for sixteen good years until yet another loss, that of her partner. Even this loss was borne successfully on the sturdy shoulders of the woman we come to admire for her willingness to share her life with us as well as its valiant content.

Lewis B. Ward-Baker, M.D.
Child psychiatrist (Ret.)
and talented actor/musician
Rochester, New York
3/30/04

PREFACE

IN THIS BOOK I HAVE WRITTEN THREE DIFFERENT KINDS OF CHAPTERS, AND I WANT TO
explain so readers are not confused. After the first chapters about the house and
business, the next seven chapters are each about a person residing at our house.
Also, after a chronological one "(Early Years)" there is one more on a person,
namely my sister. Secondly, scattered among the rest of the book are chapters
on long-term themes in my life (i.e. "My Handicap," "Music," "Depression,"
and "Spirituality"). The rest are chronological chapters. Because of the longi-
tudinal nature of some chapters and the chronological nature of others, many
incidents get mentioned twice. I've tried, in doing so, to fully discuss the incident in one place, and treat it briefly in the other, with reference notes to each
other. That way the reader will recognize the duplication.

Everyone's life is unique, so I feel safe putting that in the title, but I do
think I've had a unique confluence of themes and academics. The book is
both a confessional and a self-aggrandizement; I hope the balance of both
seems more or less reasonable. I've thoroughly enjoyed writing it; it was
therapeutic, and I feel sad that it's finished! Some parts brought back familiar sadnesses, of course.

A note about the index: I think most readers may want to browse it,
rather than look up specific items.

All the family members mentioned in this book who were older than I,
except Betsy, Carolyn, and George, are now deceased. Nevertheless, I need
to acknowledge their contributions and thank them for what they've given
me. All in all, I've enjoyed a rich life.

PROLOGUE

I WAS BORN IN THE MIDDLE OF A MIDNIGHT BLIZZARD, IN A HOSPITAL SEVERAL miles from home. Dad drove Mom in the panel delivery truck through the snow to the hospital. It was very early on St. Valentine's Day, 1928. I was named exactly after my mother, Mildred Downs Moore. My father and his family always called her Mildred, so I was Millie to them. My mother's family called her Millie, so I was Millie Jr. to them. I called myself Mooie.

Home was a homestead for a large extended family in Chatham, N.J. My father's father started building it in 1886 and enlarged it as more children came. My father, Jared, was the youngest of seven. The first three—Ralph, Ledlie, and Muriel—were born in Poughkeepsie and the rest—Anna, Gladys, Olive, and Jared—were born in that house. They all grew up there and having grown, three—Muriel and Anna, the two unmarried sisters, and Jared—lived there until 1965. Ralph died by suicide at age twenty-six, while a student at Columbia University. The rest married and then lived nearby, except for Ledlie, who with his wife moved to Massachusetts. Aunt Olive lived in Summit with Uncle Harry and their son Billie and died in 1965 in her seventies from breast cancer. Aunt Gladys lived around the corner from us with Uncle George and four children and died in her seventies from breast cancer that metastasized to her spine and paralyzed her. I last saw her in a nursing home, when she was still very communicative. There were nine paternal cousins in my generation.

My father was a florist who took over the greenhouses and wholesale business his father had built and started a retail business as well. Before this, however, he followed several paths: in college he switched from engineering to horticulture at his father's behest; he was a Boy Scout leader; a corporal in WWI; a music student at the University of Toulouse (France); an orchestral founder and conductor; and then at age thirty a florist when he decided he "should grow up" (his words to me). He married at age thirty-one.

My mother grew up as the middle of three in Jersey City. She graduated from Barnard College (part of Columbia), became a secretary at the Carnegie Education Foundation, and with her parents moved to Chatham in her late twenties, thus meeting my father. She was thirty-six when she married and stopped working. Her older brother, Fletcher, lived in Baton Rouge with Aunt Jennie, and two daughters, Edith and Janet, my only two maternal cousins. Mom's younger sister Bessie became very important to me.

I and my sister Frances were educated in the Chatham Public Schools. Chatham was a small town (5000 then), a bedroom community to New York City. Our family had lots of friends, relatives, and colleagues in Chatham. Other towns were Summit on the east and Madison on the west. I think Fran and I had a typical "small town" upbringing.

Our house was a Mecca for farther away relatives, especially ones having fallen on bad times or about to die.

The details follow.

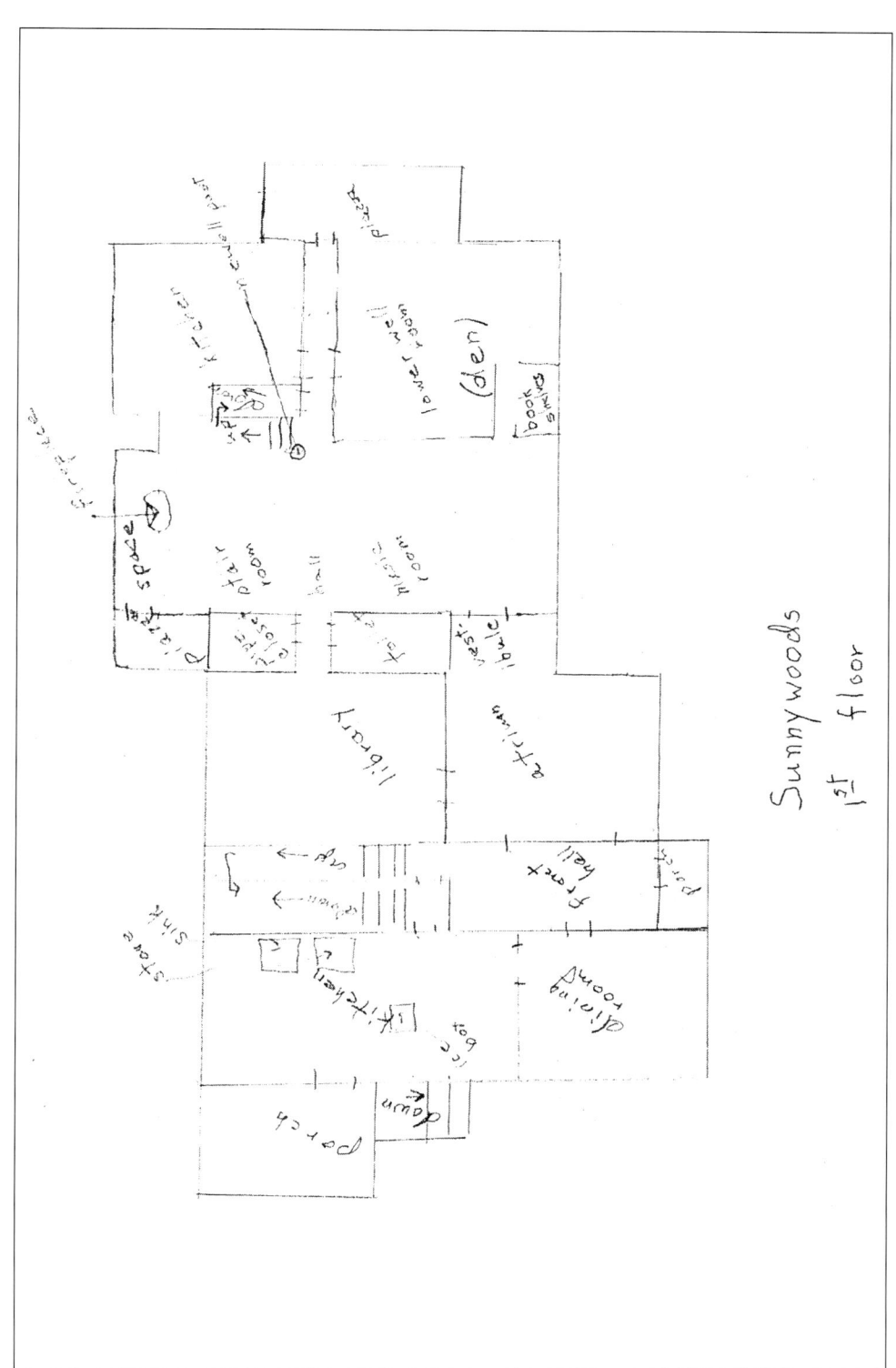

Sunnywoods
1st floor

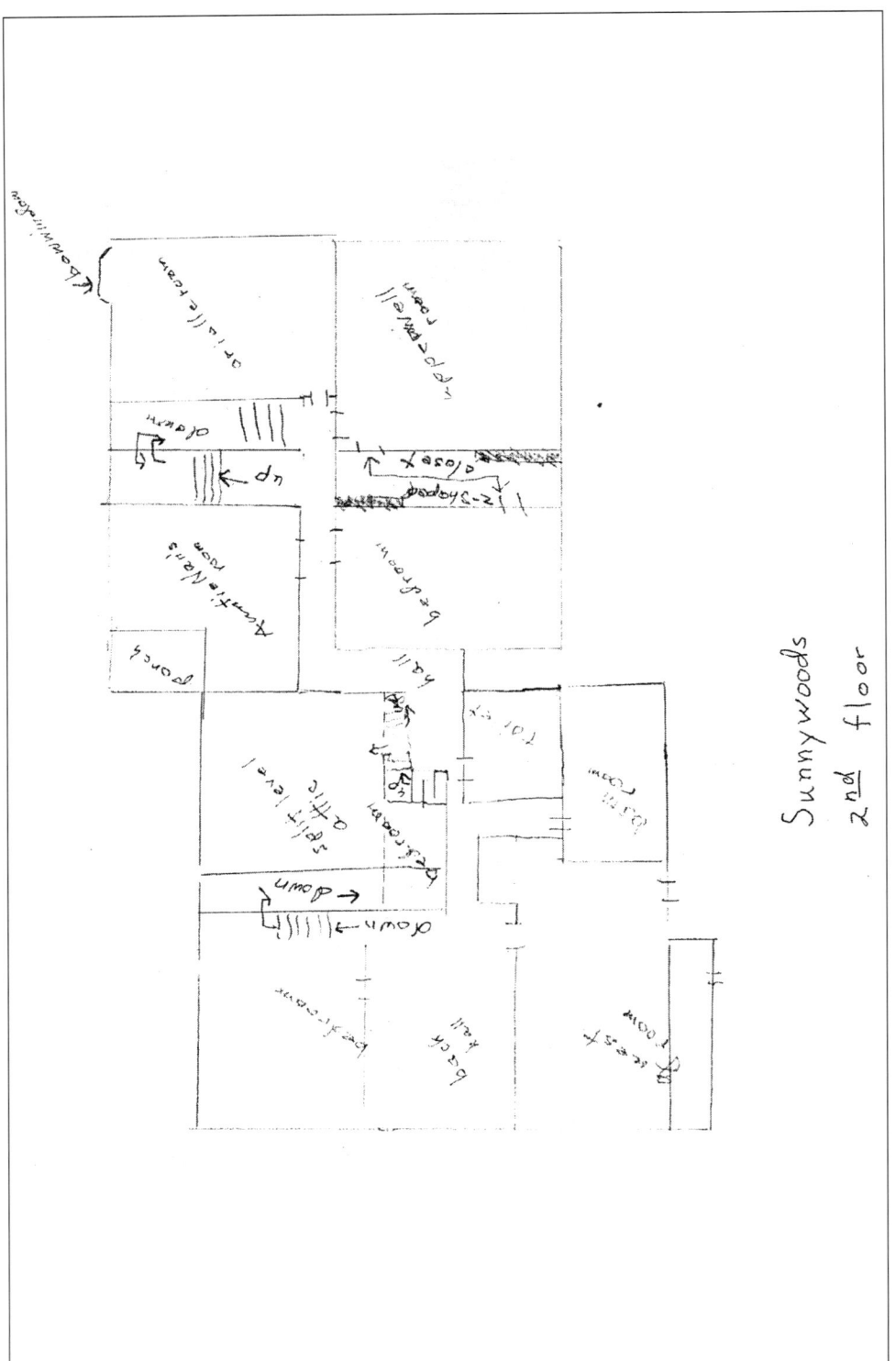

Sunnywoods
2$\underline{nd}$ floor

THAT HOUSE

THAT HOUSE WAS A FANTASTIC MANSION FOR CHILDREN TO GROW UP IN. SET ON ten acres on the side of a hill, it was built by my grandfather, in installments, as his children increased in number, but he left many areas unfinished or unrepaired. The first part, on the north (or downhill side), had four rooms in a square; and the second half, on the south (on the uphill side), had four more rooms in a square. There were two sets of stairways, one at the center of each half. The stairs in the first half were the "back stairs," and in the second half, the "main stairs" or "front stairs."

It was always hard for me to realize which direction was north or south. The south looked *up* the hill, and north downward. I felt north should be up. The hill went downward behind the house and downhill to the north; and uphill to the south.

While I was growing up, there were eight residents in the house: my paternal grandfather and grandmother and their two unmarried daughters mostly used the second half. The first half housed my parents, my sister Frances two years younger than me—and myself.

There were an outhouse and a well, but neither my sister nor I know where they were. The well was where Ralph hung himself at age twenty-six.

In the first section at the back of the house was a library. Opposite the library was the "atrium"—a sitting room—at the front of the house. Then came the front door and front hall and behind, the back stairs, both going down and up. Then came the kitchen and the dining room right off the front hall. (See diagram.)

On the second floor over the atrium was a bathroom in two parts, put in later when plumbing became possible, with a small toilet room and a somewhat larger tub, sink, and towel room. Over the library was a large bedroom which was my parents' room for several years when they were first married, and much later, after my sister got her own room. Next was the back stairs and storage area. Over the kitchen was a tiny room which served

1

various purposes, and over the dining room was another bedroom, often called the guest room. This room had a small door at the bottom of the front wall, looking down on the front porch, permitting a look to see who was there! There was no third floor over this section, but reached by more stairs was a "split-level" attic, which housed wasps, dust, and a thousand interesting things. It was over part of our parents' first bedroom.

The floor of the first part was very splintery, and we weren't allowed to go barefoot.

Onto this house Grandpa built the other four-room square. Here the floor was quite smooth. There was a kitchen, a dining room (called the "stair room") with a huge walk-around fireplace, a "music room," and a den or "lower well room," called such because, as you'll see later, it was part of a projected three-story "well." The lower well room was the earliest dining room for the grandparents and aunts. I remember one Thanksgiving dinner there. Grandpa was cutting the turkey, and I asked my mother why his hands shook so much. Later the "stair room" became their dining room. In the stair room, off the space behind the fireplace, was a walk-out deck or "back piazza," where Auntie Nan and my mother hung their clothes. The piazza needed a lot of repair, so when we went there, we had to be careful. Opposite the den was the kitchen, with the stairs between it and the stair room. At the foot of the stairs going up was a large newel post, which we think was carved, elaborately, by my grandfather. It was saved from the house and now stands in my daughter Paula's dining room.

Running from the library to the stair room was a hallway and two pipe closets. One of these was later made into a toilet room. This hallway, running through almost the length of the house, from the library between the pipe closets, between the stair room and music room, and between the kitchen and den, led to a door to the outside and a large piazza on the end of the house, which was also in poor repair. We weren't allowed out there either.

Between the music room and the atrium was a tiny little vestibule. In this tiny space was a table with ornaments and a child's rocking chair, which children were forbidden to sit in. This little chair, now recaned, is in my sitting room and the children can—and do—sit in it. Currently it has a bunch of stuffed animals in it that the children play with. We think that this vestibule room may have been meant to be the original entryroom.

On the second floor over the stair room was a bedroom, which was always my Auntie Nan's room, and a sun porch over the piazza. The story goes that when she was a child, Auntie Nan fell from the porch, and as a result was thereafter considered uneducable (although my memory is that she was a very smart woman). Opposite was another bedroom, used by different people over the years. For a long while, Frances used this room and I used the upper well room over the den. Between these two rooms was a Z-

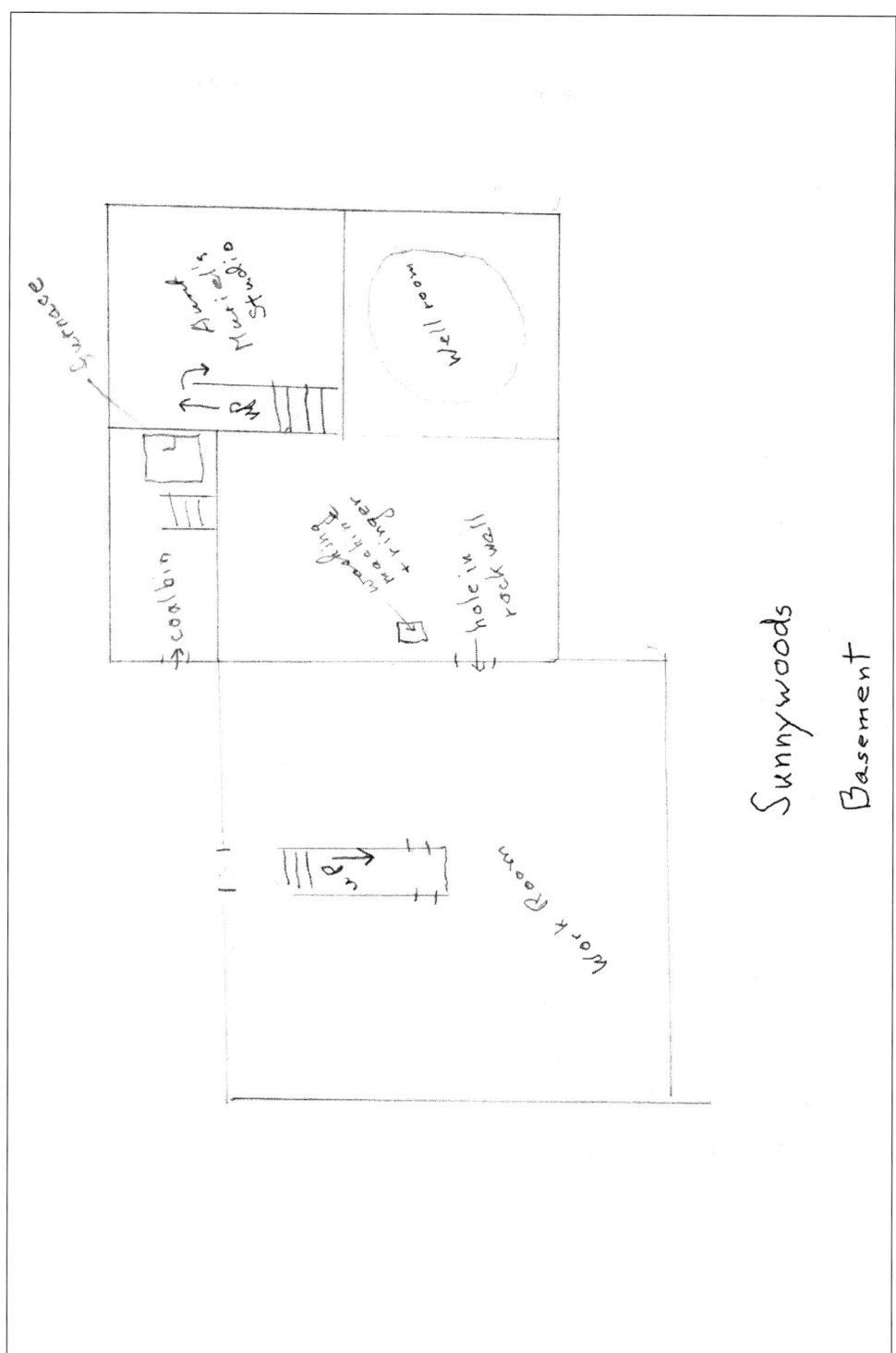

Sunnywoods
Basement

Sunnywoods
3rd floor

shaped closet which opened into both rooms at its ends. This provided a hide-and-seek secret place. The upper well room was a bedroom, my usual bedroom throughout my childhood to young adulthood.

Over the kitchen and the downstairs hallway was the master bedroom, the "orioll room," which my grandparents shared. It had a bow window looking toward the back of the property. They could just see the greenhouses from there, by looking left. I don't remember a round window (an orioll) there, nor does Fran.

There was no indoor plumbing at first. As plumbing became available, Grandpa built the two-room bathroom, and a third story over the second half of the house with two attics above it. On this third floor were two bedrooms and a half bathroom, Aunt Muriel's domain.

In the attic was the start of a huge tank for water which would serve the whole neighborhood on the downhill side, which explains the upper and lower well rooms underneath it. The tank became unnecessary before actual construction of it began because the community was growing and an artesian well was put way up on the hill above and south of the house, way beyond the cemetery.

The basement was also dug in two parts. The second half was again in two parts. Beneath the second kitchen, a room was finished off and became Aunt Muriel's art studio and school. It was accessed in good weather by a walk around the house and down some steps to a back door. In bad weather the students came through the house from the front door, through the front hall, atrium, and music room to the main stairs down to the studio.

Opposite the studio and under the upper and lower well rooms was an empty room, with a round hole about two feet deep and about ten feet in diameter, where the water tank was to have fit. For all those years, there was this crater there, with a canoe sitting in it (why?). There's probably a story, unknown to us, about that canoe.

The other half of the second half-basement was unfinished and housed laundry tubs and such. It also opened into a small stairwell down to the furnace and coal bin, under the stair room. Once, in the middle of the night, my father woke me and took me down there to see an owl (!) perched above the coal bin door.

The stone wall dividing the two halves of the basement, originally a firewall and the wall of the foundation, was broken through to the other side by a round hole one had to climb through. The rest of the basement under the first half of the house was mostly my father's workshop, where he did all kinds of repairs and made things.

All told there were eight floors, twenty-two rooms, and three attics! The second and third attics were above Aunt Muriel's room. You got up to the top one by a ladder. The *first* attic was the one between the second and third floors, split-level style, over the first half of the house.

The house was originally painted dark gray and in one windowless expanse, facing the street, my grandfather had painted a red cross (nothing to do with the American Red Cross) because of his whimsical and adventurous nature. This led to neighborhood rumors that the house had been a station on the underground railway or a hospital. Neither, of course, was true, as the house was built long after the Civil War.

Outside the foundation, around the front of the house, was a deep "moat-like" hole because it had never been filled in from when the foundation was first built. When we played in there, we found natural deposits of mica. Its separable layers made it a fun plaything.

In the front yard there was a maple tree surrounded by pachysandra ground cover, some lawn, and before the stone wall and against the little hill to the south were beautiful azaleas. When they were in full bloom, they made a very dramatic picture. Beside the drive was a fern-leaf beech, a very lovely climbing tree, which really marked our home; and at the curb by the driveway was a cedar tree. Across the apron of the driveway was the fire hydrant.

I loved to explore the house. There was always a new niche in which to hide. The bedrooms of my grandparents and aunts and the unrepaired piazzas were off-limits of course, but otherwise I went everywhere. Fran and I were imbued with the aura of "that old house."

In 1965, the house was torn down. Our neighbors, the Robinsons, bought it and built a one-story house using the same foundation. They had wanted to do that for years. Fran lived outside Philadelphia, and I in Rochester, New York, when the house was torn down. Neither of us was present. Dad and Aunt Muriel were the only residents. They moved to an apartment.

Now the property is completely leveled, according to my cousin Bill, who drives past it sometimes. I don't want to see it, but I have a beautiful copper embossed (almost three- dimensional) picture of the house and front yard made by Aunt Muriel. It shows, besides the house itself, the stone wall and the trees between that and the house. The fern-leaf beech and the cedar trees are just off to the left, but the woodsy area on the hilly part is there. This copper picture hangs in an honored place in my home.

The Sunnywoods Business

THE GREENHOUSES, BUILT AT THE BOTTOM OF THE HILL AND A LITTLE TO THE north, reached out from both sides of the potting shed. On the third side, leading to the driveway from the house, was a very large shed that trucks could drive into for loading, etc. The most action took place in the potting shed. Frances and I used to play there a lot. We played a little in certain of the greenhouses, especially the one that the steep path from the house led to and through to the potting shed. There was a male employee, Mr. Stollery, who had fun talking to and teasing us. A very clear memory occurred when I was seven, when I had just started wearing bifocals. Mr. S. called me "four-eyes," which stung and stayed with me. I never felt okay with him after that.

There were a variety of flowers in each of the houses. Especially in the fall, there were lots of chrysanthemums. Unfortunately Dad was allergic to mums and I saw that his hands in the autumn were often deep red with cracked skin. There were no desensitization treatments then; I watched him soak his hands in steaming hot water, which gave him temporary relief. He also suffered from seasonal hay fever. Many years later in life he did get— and gave himself—desensitization shots. I believe they helped the hay fever. But he no longer had to handle mums.

In another greenhouse were roses, lots of them. Grandpa practiced hybridizing them and developed the pink "Bridesmaid" rose, which was officially recognized by the rose industry. He went in to New York City by train every so often to deal in wholesale roses.

By the time Grandpa died my father had already taken over most of the business. I remember especially how Dad had to get up a few times each night to go down to the greenhouses and fire up the furnace (he had to do it at home also). It was all coal then.

During the Depression business was bad. The mortgage on the green-houses was foreclosed and the greenhouses torn down. Then houses were built on those grounds. It was a very sad time for all of us. The house was also threatened. I designed a renovation of the house, making several apartments, drawn out in great detail. Others thought about it too, but neighbors turned that down at a zoning hearing. The house was saved.

My father, with his two sisters—each of whom had certain roles in the business— decided to open a "Sunnywoods Flower Shop" downtown. It was a small but attractive place. Aunt Muriel did the signage. The same as on the truck, the logo was delicately inscribed, with the two S's large and curlicued. The store was on Passaic Avenue less than a block from Main Street.

When I was in high school, I often stopped by there after school. It was a shorter and easier walk (no hill) from school than going home. Because Dad did a lot of driving, I would wait at the store for him to drive me home.

Aunt Muriel tended the store. Though at home she was often gruff, in the store she, as I remember, was very pleasant. Frances remembers her quite differently there, that she was short-tempered with customers too, and that at one point another employee made her work only in the back room. She made beautiful bouquets and sprays. Other employees were there, especially at Christmas and other flowerful holidays like Easter. They were all exceptionally busy at those times.

The flower shop continued until Dad and his sisters were ready to retire. He sold the shop and business to a woman. It has been owned by others since. Now in 2003 the shop is still there, though moved to Main Street, with the same sign, "Sunnywoods Flower Shop."

Those Grandparents

GRANDPA WAS THE PATRIARCH AT THAT HOMESTEAD. HE WAS BORN WITH A SILVER spoon in his mouth. His father had been a very successful silversmith. We have an old picture of the Moore Silversmith Shop in New York City. The family always had servants. He was orphaned as a child and was brought up by two much older brothers and Fran thinks a sister too. They lived in New York City and then Poughkeepsie. Grandpa was an adventurer, and there were many family stories of his travels and exploits before he got married and "settled down."

He became a civil engineer after training at R.P.I. (Rensselaer Polytechnic Institute). He went to Europe, which high-class young men were expected to do. One story was that he "almost" built the Brooklyn Bridge. He did build the first elevator in a Denver "high-rise" of six stories. At the Oregon-Washington State border, he walked around a pole several times so he could say that he'd been to Washington six times. He was involved in many Western stories.

He returned East and married Caroline Frances Belcher, whom he had claimed as his future bride when she was a baby in a cradle. She was fourteen years younger than he. After three children were born in Poughkeepsie, and they first looked at the ten acre property in Chatham, she exclaimed, "Oh what a sunny woods!" and that became the lasting name of the whole place and whole business. He called her "Ducky," and she solved all his problems—finding lost keys and papers, etc. One time I heard him scream, "Ducky, Ducky, where are my accounts?" and she responded immediately in a very soft voice with the solution.

He was one of the founders of St. Paul's Episcopal Church in Chatham, which nurtured all of our family.

Grandma was largely a nonentity to me. She was very passive and quiet, saved Grandpa from his tantrums, and paid little or no attention to my sister and me, except we ritually kissed her, Grandpa, and the aunts goodnight as we went through the music room where they sat evenings, on our way to the main stairway to our bedroom.

Frances and I, for several years, shared this bedroom, the "upper well room," next to the (master) orioll bedroom. My sister has told me—since our becoming adults—that Grandpa was verbally very abusive to Grandma while they were going to bed. She heard them through the wall. He did the yelling, she said nothing. I don't remember this, whether because I've repressed it or got to sleep earlier than my sister.

When I was very little, Grandma had a little and quite old dog named Shad. I don't remember him, but Mom, who was a dog lover, said he was very sweet. He's in one of the photos of me as a toddler.

Fran and I had little or no relationship with either grandparent, except Fran remembers Grandpa teasing her in the dark hallway with his cane, frightening her. Both of them were very old by the time we were growing up. I remember how, when she was developing Alzheimer's but still talking, Grandma's word memory became a serious problem for her.

After Grandpa had built enough of the house to live in, and between his further building projects, he built the eleven-range greenhouses, with a potting shed and a couple of employees. He was in the rose-growing business. He developed the Bridesmaid Rose, which received good notice in the rose business and is now considered an "antique rose."

The greenhouses were at the bottom of the hill behind the house and a little to the north. The road curved down like an omega, but the footpath was direct and quite steep. One time, when Grandpa was pretty old, my sister and I, while playing below with Jimmy, a neighbor boy, watched him from across the meadow as he laboriously climbed the path with his cane. He sat for a few minutes on a halfway bench, then continued up the hill. He stopped briefly, and then suddenly tumbled over and over down the steep drop-off from the path into some bushes. Jimmy ran to him while Fran and I ran to get help. Grandpa was not injured, but for a few hours it was an exciting family crisis.

My father eventually took over the business. Grandpa lived to ninety-two. Shortly after Grandpa's last train trip to NYC, he got pneumonia, then known as the "old man's friend." Before antibiotics it allowed a quick and relatively painless death. Fran remembers that he was giving a speech at the church parish house, collapsed in the middle, and had to be carried out.

He lay dying in the master bedroom. The whole family, including many who did not actually live there, gathered and sat at the other side of the room, in front of the bow window. Frances and I were instructed separately to go up to him and say goodbye. When I stood there by him, he blinked his eyes, so I knew he heard me. I was ten years old.

He died sometime after Fran and I went to bed. That whole scene is still very vivid in my memory. I remember Uncle Ledlie the next day, sitting with his head down on the first steps of Aunt Muriel's stairway, right outside the orioll room.

After Grandpa died, Grandma seemed to gradually deteriorate. The family thought she had a stroke, but I believe it was Alzheimer's disease. Auntie Nan was her caretaker for almost ten years and I remember her walking Grandma through the house several times a day to visit my mother in her kitchen. She was no longer talking and needed total supervision. She was sometimes incontinent in our sitting room (the atrium) as she walked.

Finally, she was totally bedridden. When I was home for the 1947 summer from college, she died, at eighty-seven. The idea of death froze me a little, but I can't say I felt any grief. Only pity for both her and Auntie Nan. Both Grandma and Grandpa were buried in Greenwood Cemetery in Brooklyn. I think I remember Grandpa's funeral, but I didn't attend Grandma's.

Some years later I received from my cousin Ted (Carolyn and Betsy's oldest brother who worked on the family's genealogy) a "Journal of Caroline F. Moore." Reading this was astounding to me and gave me a totally different picture of Grandma. It is written in a very clear hand, with graceful lines. The first fifteen pages were evidently written in Poughkeepsie. They tell about the first three children, Ralph, Ledlie, and Muriel: their births, baptisms, and a great many of their childish sayings. The eleventh and twelfth pages show tracings of their hands, apparently made in 1886. She speaks once of the house they're going to build.

Then there's a two-year hiatus, the book "lost," probably because of the move. The next pages, now in Chatham, include some catch-up information about Anna's and Gladys' births and baptisms. Both Ralph and Ledlie had had some serious illnesses, which resulted in all night vigils for both her and "Papa." Papa is mentioned frequently as lovingly taking part in their play and conversations. Three and a half pages comprise this part and include handprints of all five children. Her next entry is in 1889; the next five and a half pages continue about the five and begin to include some drawings by them. She speaks of the plans to build on to the house.

In 1890, she mentions Olive's birth, and the fact that they had had servants but right then they were gone and she is doing the work alone until the building is done. (By the time I was born, there were no more servants.) She also mentions playing the piano and hopes Ledlie's musicality will grow so she'll have a companion. She speaks of some of their faults, such as Muriel's temper, and hopes they'll outgrow them; also their accomplishments. Then Muriel's drawings begin to appear, with increasing skill. In 1893, Jared's birth is announced. The children are taught to darn their stockings, make beds, and learn Bible verses. She writes out a story she made up for them, with a good father, a bad man, and a happy ending. For a while they were all sick, and she didn't write. Ledlie, now eleven, is in the church choir and "is quite wrapped up in Jared, and I am so glad." She gives all their heights in 1899.

Auntie Nan

Grandpa Moore

Grandma Moore

Grandma Downs

The next entry skips to 1902. It mentions Jared taking music lessons, no doubt from his mother. In 1903, Ledlie, now twenty-one and a student in engineering at Lehigh University, started working for the summer with the Chicago Great Western Railway and traveled to Minnesota. Ralph had started at Columbia University, planning to enter the ministry. Gladys is starting at Cooper Union. "Jared is my comfort too. I can always count upon his love and willingness to help." He shows talent in constructing and building and in music at age ten. The whole manuscript is written with obvious lovingness.

The next to last entry is, "On February 27,1906 our dear boy Ralph was taken from us, and is we hope and trust waiting for us in our Home above cared for by our Heavenly Father." She doesn't mention the suicide. Jared was thirteen.

The last entry, a year later, is about Ledlie's graduation in 1907 from Lehigh as a mining engineer and now he is in Mexico. "Our home seems to be gradually breaking up, and it makes me long for our real Home where there will be no more parting." Jared is fourteen. There's no more. I feel like crying.

The Breadwinner and Guide

Jared, my father, was the last-born to Frank and Caroline Moore, in 1893, in the big house in Chatham, New Jersey. He went to school in a one-room schoolhouse and in high school played on the football team, where his presence was necessary because there were only twelve boys in the high school. His parents were loving and devoted but were very strict and taught the children basic self-care: all had to darn their own stockings, iron their shirts, make their beds, and keep everything neat. One time, for some infraction, Jared's father beat him down behind the barn. Another time Jared dropped a heavy iron on his foot while he was ironing his shirt and broke a toe. He never told his parents, fearing a reprimand, and the toe healed on its own.

He was musically and mechanically inclined, taking piano lessons as a child and building things. He attended Lehigh University, planning to be an engineer as his father and one older brother (Ledlie, ten years older) had done. But after the first year, his father decided Jared was the only one who could take over his floral business—greenhouses, roses, wholesale, and retail. He required Jared to transfer to Rutgers University where he could major in agriculture (horticulture was not available). He was amenable to this, his philosophy being the specific path is not as relevant as how one walks it. For his senior thesis, he wrote about a pest to the cattleya orchid, called the cattleya fly.

After he graduated, he enlisted in the U.S. Army and was a corporal in France during WWI. He was close behind the front lines, doing measurements, and could see and be threatened by the enemy. He was a "forward observer," having to note where the enemy was and where his company's shells were landing. He became an unlabelled pacifist. He was in France two years, one year after the Armistice. He stayed with a family, learned to speak French, and took music courses at the University of Toulouse, learning to play the oboe and to conduct an orchestra. He was repatriated back to the USA after that year.

Dad — age 24

Dad — age 50's

At home then he founded the Sunnywoods Orchestra, which for a while was actually two orchestras—an adult one in which two of his older sisters, Muriel (viola) and Olive (violin) played, and a student orchestra. There still was no music program in the public school.

These full-fledged orchestras drew for membership on Chatham and nearby towns. They practiced in our living room (the atrium), where I listened to them from ten days of age. (See more about this in the chapter "Music, My Solace.")

He founded the Chatham chapter of the American Legion. During the early 1920s, he was also a Boy Scout leader, establishing the first Chatham troop, and enjoyed taking the boys on elaborate camping trips. He played chess whenever he could, teaching me to play it when I was four. At some point after retirement, he started to play a lot of chess with correspondents, by postcard.

After learning the flower business and gradually starting to take it over, he married my mother in 1924 when he was thirty-one and she thirty-six. It was August 31, I was told, a very hot and muggy day. They were married in the Congregational Church across the street.

They lived in the bedroom under the split-level attic. They had a hot plate but no other accessories. It was a long time before his father gave them other rooms at the north end downstairs to use. Some time around my birth in 1928 they were given the first-built kitchen (which at first served as both kitchen and dining room) and the front room, which later became our dining room, beside the front hall. They were also given the upper well room at the far south corner for my bedroom, right next door to my grandparents' room. When my sister was born in 1929, she was put in my room also. Some time around then, our parents moved into the next room, the one with the Z-shaped closet opening into both.

Dad's main dicta that I took to heart were, "Give your employer full-time hard work;" "Don't smoke;" "Don't drink alcohol;" "Keep your promises and integrity at a high level." His integrity was impeccable. He was unflappable. As teenager, I once pretended to smoke a cigarette, and his only response was "Good scissors!"

During the Great Depression, Dad had a hard time keeping the business going. We always had good food to eat, but clothes and other niceties slipped away. He was supporting the whole household, except for Aunt Muriel's income. (See the chapter "Ahead of Her Time.")

Finally, after my grandfather's death in 1938, the greenhouses were foreclosed and torn down and houses built there and across the meadow. It was a sad time. The orchestra also petered out, partly because school started a music program, and partly because of the war.

When the greenhouses went, so did the wholesale part of the business. My father and Aunt Muriel, after her retirement from teaching art, opened a flower shop downtown. Auntie Nan had become the business' bookkeeper, doing that work every evening at home. At Christmas time, which was very hectic, I helped in the store with all transactions and kept it all on track. I also received the many phone calls and orders.

During the Depression Dad also joined the WPA (Works Progress Administration, started as part of President Roosevelt's New Deal) Orchestra, playing the oboe, for which he was paid. I remember how he had to make the reeds, scraping them so carefully to get the right timbre. I greatly enjoyed being with and watching him in whatever he was doing. He then played in the Summit Symphony and others, giving it up only when he was about eighty.

During WWII, he worked evening shifts at a manufacturing plant building PT boats and later as a punch-card manager at Bethlehem Steel. He carpooled with a friend because of the gas rationing. I remember him turning off the engine to coast down a hill to save gas. Also during the war he was a volunteer sky watcher. He went several miles at night to the tower to watch for and report all planes, to warn of any enemy ones. One time I went with him in the middle of the night. It was exciting for me, but we saw no planes that time. I admired my dad greatly and I wanted to join him in anything he did.

Financially then we did somewhat better. Even after my grandfather's death in 1938, my grandmother's in 1947, my mother's in 1955, and Auntie Nan's in the early 1960s, and even after my leaving for graduate school in 1950 and Frances' marriage in 1952, he was still supporting Aunt Muriel, although she did have savings from her working career.

In 1965, the house was torn down. Dad and Aunt Muriel, the only ones left, moved to an apartment. He sold the flower shop but took a job with another florist and retired from that years later. After retirement he became very active at St. Paul's Episcopal Church.

In the early 1960s, about age seventy, he bought a modern new oboe from a player in the Rochester Philharmonic while visiting Rochester. One of my cousins wrote me that he thought my dad was being too self-indulgent since he was so old. I wrote back defending Dad's right to use his money as he wished and said he had many more years of playing.

Dad and Frances, her husband Dave, and all their family went to France in 1973. They retraced the route he had taken during and after WWI. Fran wrote about it in an essay that was published in the *New York Times*. Dad enjoyed the trip immensely.

He was still active in an orchestra, playing correspondence chess with a dozen or more friends and relatives, and working as a crossing guard for schoolchildren. Around age eighty, he finally got dentures. His teeth had always been bad but unfortunately this destroyed his oboe embouchure (it apparently affected how he used his lips) and he could no longer play. He

Dad — age 92

was a very even-tempered person and adapted to this loss better than I. I felt very sorry about it.

He started Brailling books for the blind, under supervision of the Library of Congress, and later received a plaque of commendation from the Library, which I have.

After Aunt Muriel died in the 1970s, the family started holding family reunions on or near his May birthday at my sister's house outside Philadelphia every five years. About fifty cousins and offspring usually came, some from California and New Mexico. At one of them, Dad and my cousin Ted (Carolyn's and Betsy's oldest brother) played a chess game outdoors, moving the people about on a pretend lawn board. At the first reunion, the cake featured the first musical phrase of Schubert's "Unfinished Symphony" (to me, symbolic of him because he was still growing and unfinished), an oboe, and a chess piece in the corners.

He was still driving at that time, but my cousin Bill (the same Billie that Fran and I played with as kids) who still lived in Summit and alone, took more and more responsibility for him, since Fran and I both lived far away. He and Dad had an ambivalent relationship with many disagreements, but each had only each other and they both thrived. Dad finally gave up the crossing guard job and driving in his nineties. He continued chess, receiving several trophies, and Brailling. In 1993, when he was 100, we held the last family reunion.

In January 1995, I got a call from a doctor at Overlook Hospital (Summit) that Dad had had a heart attack. Frances remembers that she called me first, but I don't recall that. I was at Beth Jelsma's house, preparing to attend a concert with her, when Lou called me from home saying this doctor at Overlook Hospital wanted to talk to me about my dad. I made the call and received the news. His heart had been zapped once with the defibrillator, and the doctor wanted my permission to not do it again. I said after a moment's reaction to all this to let him go. Bill was present and had called 911 after Dad told him on the phone that he hadn't gotten out of bed. Dad was mentally active and physically too, right to the end.

Beth and I went to the concert, but at intermission I decided to leave and check out flights to Newark. Both Fran and I got there the next morning. Paula, Lorna, and Lynn (my daughters and Paula's spouse) arrived soon after. Bill joined us for conferences with the funeral director. This time, I really participated. But I still didn't grieve as much as one might expect. Lou came a day or two later. Izzie also came. Wally didn't come— he explained later that his back was bad. He had, in fact, had a good relationship with my dad. When Dad had visited Rochester, he and Wally had played music together, Wally on accordion, Dad on oboe.

After the funeral, Frances and I were in Dad's apartment doing some sorting and discarding. Dad's Public Health nurse, Beverly Wolfe, was there also. She had taken care of Dad for several years, helping him bathe and supervising his food and meds, and was very fond of him. She had been a tremendous support, and probably it was she (and also Bill) who helped him live so long. As she was working in the apartment, she was fighting back tears. It would have been a good opportunity for me to give her a hug and some comforting. But I was not feeling grief then and didn't. I deeply regret not responding to her sadness.

Seven of the nine cousins were there for the funeral and the drive to Greenwood Cemetery in Brooklyn. Frank, who lived north of Brooklyn, was supposed to meet us for the grave ceremony, but didn't get there. Louise, his sister in California, died the same year of ovarian cancer. George (Betsy and Carolyn's older brother) gave Fran and me a letter Dad wrote to him on the morning before his death. Dad had lived a glorious life.

Mildred and Mommy

Mildred and Daddy

THE STOIC

MY MOTHER GREW UP WITH BOYS. AN OLDER BROTHER WAS NAMED FLETCHER. Three brothers, closer to her and her sister's ages, lived next door, and she told Frances and me that they played together just about every day. Her sister Bessie was four years younger than she and her brother Fletcher was four years older.

So my mother knew all about boys. I don't understand why or how she transferred to me a fear of boys and men. But I have a theory—two later circumstances fit it. My father has told me that when they were married, Mom already knew all about sex and taught him. Also, whenever we visited Uncle Fletcher's family, either in Chatham or Baton Rouge, Louisiana, I was disturbed by a habit of his: he constantly had his hand in his pocket, jingling coins or keys. I believe Mom never left either of us (Fran and me) alone with him. My theory, unproven, is that as teens Fletcher played sex games with Mom. Consequently she was especially concerned that we not get into a similar situation and in instructing us, overdid her concern.

When she was at Barnard College, she spent one or two summers with Dr. Franz Boaz, the great anthropologist, at his family's summer place in the Adirondacks, as his secretary. He taught Ruth Benedict and Margaret Meade at Barnard. Mom revered him and learned and repeated to me and my sister many Native American stories and myths. Unfortunately, I don't remember any of them.

After graduation, she worked at the Carnegie Education Foundation in New York City as a secretary. She made many friends at both Barnard and Carnegie, some of whom I got to know. One time she took Frances and me to visit Carnegie and she showed us off to her former colleagues.

She and her parents moved from Jersey City to Chatham while she was working at Carnegie. I don't know why they moved, but that was when she met my father. Mom's father was blind from kidney disease. For years, Mom was his guide. They both worked in New York, he as an engineer. Mom and he both commuted to New York daily by train. He and Uncle Fletcher were both graduates of Columbia University. My father has told me that he was very fond of Mom's father. He died some time while Mom and Dad were engaged. Dad was walking with her and teared up in grief, but he hid it from her. Late in life he told me he now regretted not letting her know his feelings.

They were married in 1924 when she was thirty-six. She wanted children very much. She and he were given, by my grandparents, the upstairs room (sort of a double room) to live in. The only accessory she had was a hot plate. Apparently the plumbing was not complete upstairs so she had to carry buckets of water upstairs several times a day. She had two pregnancies that miscarried, supposedly because of that straining. She got pregnant again, with me. This time she went to live with her mother and sister, who now were in Westchester County. She thought that might avoid another miscarriage. I don't know how close she called it timewise, but she was back with my dad by the time I was born. She was thirty-nine, and when my sister was born, she was forty.

About that time my grandparents finally gave them two—and later a third—rooms downstairs including a kitchen, and one upstairs at the other end of the house for me. Later Mom and Dad moved their bedroom to the one next to mine. These now were the two rooms with the Z-shaped closet between. Some time in those early years, Mom developed rheumatoid arthritis, mostly in her knees and hands. I remember her struggle to climb stairs. She was slow and awkward in all her movements. She received gold injections from Dr. Eckhardt in Madison. I'm not sure how much they actually helped. Steroids had not yet been discovered. Dad drove her weekly in the truck to her appointment. I learned much later that Dr. Eckhardt's alma mater was Cornell University Medical College, which became mine too.

Mom tried once to learn to drive, when Frances and I were about seven or eight. Not having a babysitter, Fran and I were in the panel delivery truck too. Dad had installed two folding chairs behind the front seats for us. For the driving lesson my father was in the passenger seat. He instructed Mom to turn on the ignition, to put it in gear, and move the car. Of course the car lurched quite a bit. Frances and I started screaming, from fear that she would have us all in an accident. It seemed just not right for anyone other than Dad to drive. She abruptly ended the lesson and there were no more. She never did learn to drive.

Although in college she had majored in math, she was very interested in history and geography. This was manifested later during her membership in the Legion Auxiliary (as a veteran, Dad had founded the Chatham chapter of the American Legion). One year she was chairman of the international committee and created a beautiful scrapbook about South America, the topic for that year. She had a close college friend, whom I called Miss Jo, who became a nurse and went to South America as a missionary. So my mother didn't see her for years, but was really devastated when she learned that Miss Jo had committed suicide after many years in Brazil. I think that scrapbook was a memorial to Miss Jo.

She did a lot of volunteer work. One I remember best was her being an election registrar. She claimed she liked chicken necks and always took one when it was passed. My Dad has wondered if she was actually saving others from having to deal with it. I think she was just being frugal, as she was about every purchase.

She taught me a number of dicta: 1) Be nice to others; 2) Be kind, compassionate, and generous; 3) Don't talk much or ask questions; if you listen you'll probably get the answer; 4) Don't smoke, drink alcohol, or have sex; 5) Don't complain or argue; 6) Keep your promises. Regarding sex, she said "not before marriage," but somehow I didn't take in that part, only the general dictum. She also said, "Don't show your feelings," which is opposite to what my therapists taught, but stood me in good stead in practicing psychotherapy. She really taught me to be passive.

When I was in college she began complaining of a constant metallic taste in her mouth. Now, a work-up would include X-rays of the GI tract, but then it was ignored. When she finally developed more severe symptoms, she was advised to have an operation. This was while I was a first-year medical student. They found colon cancer and removed it but said it had been stuck to the abdominal wall, so there were very likely some cancer cells left.

One time after one of the surgeries, we were going into the house after a ride. Dad and Mom walked together and I was behind. I saw Dad put his arm around her waist. That was the only affectionate gesture I ever saw in them, other than goodbye pecks. Fran says she saw many more such gestures, about which I'm glad. My mother knew she was going to die from the cancer. One time, when she was beginning to get really sick and was sleeping in the corner (guest) room, she said to me, "I'm going to die, aren't I?" I answered "Yes." I stayed with her for a bit, but she seemed to not want to talk more.

Even then, I still retained my adolescent feelings of hostility toward her. I wish that by that time I had gotten over that. She died in my bed in June at the end of my third year of medical school. I was home from school, but I didn't want to stay there. Between her death and her funeral, I went back to school for a lab job I had, then went home again for the funeral. During all that time, I felt numb. Writing this chapter and the one on medical school, which tells more about her death, has helped to reduce those hostile feelings.

AHEAD OF HER TIME

AUNT MURIEL WAS THE OLDER SPINSTER, THE THIRD-BORN OF THE SEVEN. SHE WAS born in the early 1880s in Poughkeepsie, but grew up and lived most of her life in that house. She was a large woman, dressed in the fashions of the thirties that she sewed herself, gray-haired with a bun. She made all her own clothes. She was very heavy, and I can still hear her coming, each footfall a "boom" echoing through that house. Fran and I were scared of her. She had a very loud voice and didn't hesitate to let her scorn or disapproval be heard. She rarely smiled, was a prude, and was not child-oriented. It was only much later that I really realized her positive attributes.

She was a person ahead of the times. In our family, she was the first woman of her generation to buy and drive a car; travel by rail and ocean boat without a family chaperone; the first to get a permanent (possibly the second—Frances thinks Aunt Gladys also got permanents); the first and only one to really make a career for herself; the only one to invite a male friend to live for a while in that house when he was down and out.

She was an artist. She painted with oils (I still have three of her paintings), sculpted with clay (I have a set of three boys playing marbles—there are several copies of this sculpture, now in various grandchildren's houses—and a plaque embossed with a picture of Mom's dog Gypsy); made copper plaques (I have one, embossed, of the house); and sculpted jewelry from pewter and colorful stones. She attended and graduated from Cooper Union, where she studied art. She traveled across country to Montana, where she got some of her art training and taught, and traveled to Europe to visit the great museums. She gave me, as a teenager, a book of paintings by a Spanish artist (Velazquez). She taught art in a public school in Madison, the next town, and taught classes privately in her studio in our basement.

Regarding Aunt Muriel's teaching studio, Fran remembers that it first was on the third floor, in one of those two rooms of hers. I remember it only after she renovated and used the basement studio. This room was about twelve by twelve, curtained off by scrimshaw from the rest of the basement, behind the stairs going up, and to screen off the well room. The studio had a number of windows and was well-lighted. Half a dozen easels were scattered about, and a table for clay work was before a window. The year I was in second grade my parents decided I shouldn't continue her art lessons because I was having eye trouble. I used to go halfway down her stairs and watch the lesson going on. Once while there I told her that I wished I had been denied the piano lessons rather than art—mostly because with piano I had to practice. She grunted and continued the lesson. I restarted lessons the next year.

We had, at that time, a lovely German shepherd named Fritzie, who before my mother got her, had been abused and couldn't be trusted with strangers who hadn't been properly introduced. On one occasion, a girl of about twelve, one of Aunt Muriel's students, came in through the front door for her art lesson. Unfortunately, Fritzie, who was supposed to be confined to our dining room, got out and attacked and bit her. Of course there was a major commotion, and I saw the girl sitting and shaking in the atrium, another exciting crisis. Fritzie, of whom I was very fond, had to be put down soon after. It was a very sad time. The girl was not seriously hurt, but that whole episode has remained vividly with me.

Aunt Muriel played the viola and was part of the orchestra my father founded, which practiced in the atrium.

Aunt Muriel also kept an easel going in the room next to her bedroom. For my college graduation she gave me a painting she did of a photo I had taken on a trip down through the mid-Atlantic states. It was of a waterwheel before a small hill with my father strolling on the hill and a pond in the foreground. I still enjoy looking at it.

After she retired from teaching art, she became an important part of the Sunnywoods business. She ran the store downtown and made up beautifully artistic bouquets and sprays.

One reason she always appeared gruff was that she had the "Moore mouth," which in repose has its ends pulled down. Dad, Frances, and I also have it. Since being aware of it, I've tried to smile a lot to counteract the image.

Aunt Muriel belonged to the "Anthroposophical Society." She tried to explain it to me once, but I was not able to understand what it stood for. Occasionally she made an all-day trip, driving to Spring Valley, New York, where the society had its headquarters. She evidently had a physician there, because Spring Valley had something to do with finding her breast lump and getting the mastectomy. Once when I was a teen, as a birthday gift, she took me to New York to see a play, *Faust*, by Goethe. That performance also had something to do with the Anthroposophical Society. For the play, the stage was quite dark, and I couldn't see any action. Voices intoned their lines in deep, ghostly ways, so I could not understand them. For me it was pretty boring. Aunt Muriel didn't try to talk about it afterward. Maybe she had trouble understanding it, too. Anyway, I was glad she didn't say anything as I didn't know what I could say. As an adult, I studied *Faust* with Gounod's music. I think Aunt Muriel loved me.

She was also the first in our family to have a mastectomy for breast cancer, before I was born. Breast cancer has been a theme in my family. Late in her life, she had a second one. After surgery, she did okay for several years, but ultimately it got to the rest of her body and she succumbed in the hospital (Overlook) in her eighties. By that time, I was fond of her although I rarely saw her, as I was grown up and lived elsewhere. I saw her once in the hospital and I kissed her, and she smiled. That was not long before she died.

THE CARETAKER

THE ONE TIME THAT AUNTIE NAN HAD TO BABYSIT MY SISTER AND ME WAS WHEN we were about eight and ten. Since we had been born, this was our parents' only date until we went to college, so having them gone was an exciting adventure. They had decided to see *The Chocolate Soldier* at the Paper Mill Playhouse. At that time Frances and I shared the upper well room, at the top of the main stairs. We went to bed like good little girls, but suddenly we felt free, and we talked as we often did, but for an unusually long time. Finally, after an hour or so, Auntie Nan came reluctantly up the stairs, opened our door, and said harshly, "Don't you want your parents to have a good time?" This was a terrible rebuke, quite guilt-producing. We immediately quieted down and after feeling bad for a while, we went to sleep. She never babysat us again; I think my parents felt very guilty too after Auntie Nan told them what happened. There were enough guilt trips to go around in both parents and kids. I'm sure my parents never tried again to persuade her. It was a big deal.

I don't know why we called her Auntie Nan; all the other cousins called her Aunt Anna. Auntie Nan was a dowdy woman with gray hair who (other than that night) was always friendly to Fran and me. I learned after growing up that she was a very important confidante to my sister and played an important role in Fran's emotional development. With me, she had a kind of topical relationship. I was a co-birdwatcher. She kept a feeder full outside her kitchen window, and often came looking for me, "Come quick! There's a cardinal on the feeder!" or "...woodpecker..." and I rushed to see. Once there was even a scarlet tanager. This was a major influence for me, as I became an avid birdwatcher much later in life.

I have another special memory of her. She was the homemaker and cook for her end of the house (grandparents, her, and Aunt Muriel). Occasionally she would make homemade bread and then come over to our end of the house to offer us some. The aroma and taste of freshly baked bread was salivatingly wonderful! Whenever I smell it now, I always think of Auntie Nan.

She was easily hurt. One time when she walked Grandma, who at that time had stopped talking, to my mother's kitchen, she and I got into the beginning of a debate over whether eggs that were difficult to shell were fresh or not fresh. She quickly turned Grandma around and walked away. Mom said, "Don't argue with her. She can't take it."

She had her own garden a ways down the hill on the left of the drive and spent a lot of time there until my grandmother got too ill to be left alone.

She had sinus trouble, and Dad drove her weekly to her doctor in Summit to have her sinuses lavaged.

One year, before I can remember, she applied to accept a Fresh Air Child for a week. She was basically broad-minded, liked children, and wanted to do good. He came, but it lasted about two days. She sent him back because his behavior was impossible to tolerate, and she had no idea how to handle him. She never tried that again.

She was the bookkeeper for the Sunnywoods business and spent every evening in the library after Grandpa could no longer do it. She was very bright and well-informed, even though she had been cheated out of some education because of that childhood fall from her sun porch.

Whenever relatives came to stay at our house for a time because they were sick or depressed, which happened a number of times, she (and/or my mother) was their caretaker, as well as for *her* mother. I will say more of this phenomenon in a later chapter, but with her mother she spent almost ten years caring for her every minute. Once she tried putting her in a local nursing home. She left Grandma there only one day, as she saw that Grandma was not getting the degree of care that she (Auntie Nan) could and did give her.

The year Auntie Nan died, in the early sixties, I went to Chatham to see her. Because she could no longer climb the stairs, she was bedded in the library, next to the pipe closet bathroom. She had had a "breakdown" in early adulthood (probably depression), which caused her to withdraw from Cooper Union, where Muriel and Gladys went. At my visit, I went to her, sitting on the makeshift bed, and she asked me, "Is what's happening to me the same as that time?" I knew what she meant—the "nervous breakdown." I reassured her that it wasn't, but I now wish that I had encouraged that conversation to go longer. She had ovarian cancer and really needed a conversation about it. She died a week or so before her birthday. I had bought for her birthday a beautiful encyclopedic bird book and donated it to the Chatham Public Library (now The Library of the Chathams) in her memory. I grieved very little for her.

Both Aunt Muriel and Auntie Nan were buried in Greenwood Cemetery in Brooklyn. I attended neither funeral.

My Confidante

My mother's sister, Aunt Bessie, a cataloguing librarian in a Westchester County library, did not live with us but visited nearly every weekend and holiday, especially after her mother came to live with us. She was my favorite aunt, my confidante and friend, who I often wished had been my mother. I always enjoyed her visits.

She was unmarried, was somewhat shy, and prone to depression. I learned from my mother that before I was born, while on holiday at a resort in New England, she had taken an overdose of pills and was severely sedated. Friends there walked her for several hours to try to keep her awake until she recovered. Several summers she and I spent a week or two at that New England resort or at the Antlers Inn in the Pocanos, just relaxing.

For birthdays and Christmas gifts she invariably gave me a book, of which she as a librarian had a very large choice. The most memorable and influential book I ever received, when I was ten or twelve, was *The World at My Finger Tips*, an autobiography by a blind man, Karsten Ohnstad, who triumphed over his handicap. It was a powerful inducement to me to live with and overcome my handicap. Another was *Little People Who Became Great*.

When I was about twelve, I visited her at her apartment. She helped me look more feminine. As a child, my eyebrows were continuous above my nose. She showed me how to pluck out the excess hairs. She was more up-to-date than my mother was. I visited several times. She would take me to the library with her, and I would sit and read Mary Roberts Rinehart mysteries. I loved them.

For my high school graduation gift, she gave me a year's subscription to see and hear the New York Philharmonic at Carnegie Hall every Sunday afternoon with her and often with a friend of hers. Each week I took the Lackawanna train to Hoboken, where I met her. I was, from very early, an avid music lover, and this expanded my musical love and knowledge beyond measure. Maestro Bruno Walter conducted. I remember in particular Tschaikowsky's *Fifth* and *Sixth*

Aunt Bessie

Symphonies, Brahms' *First Symphony*, and Tschaikowsky's *Violin Concerto*, which I think was played by Jascha Heifetz.

Sometimes I felt bored listening, because I was used to doing homework or reading at home during the radio concerts. That year was when I spent nights at the elderly lady's house (See the "In-Between Year") and came to the conclusion that I wasted much time and would immediately stop that. I think that was why I felt bored at the theater.

On one occasion we and Aunt Bessie's friend were talking about our love of music. Aunt Bessie was saying how much pleasure it was to know technical points about it, to which I heartily agreed. Her friend, I thought oddly, said she'd rather not know those things because it would interfere with her enjoyment. I was fond of this friend, but that really puzzled me. I have always, in many ways, been guided by a need to know the complete truth.

After the concert we had tea or dinner, going to a different international restaurant each time. I remember in particular the Russian Tea Room, which was popular and for some reason finally closed in 2002. I remember the very tasty borscht.

Aunt Bessie taught me social things I should have known, sometimes quite embarrassing. One time we were sitting in a large family group. Ruth Webb (see "Barnard College") was on the far side from me, near a window. My watch was reflecting light from the window and I discovered I could move the beam of light. I focused it on Ruth, hoping to get her attention. She fidgeted to get the beam out of her eye but wasn't going to notice me. Aunt Bessie saw what I was doing and reprimanded me, and I stopped. She caught me a number of times when I was being annoying in some way.

When I was at college at Barnard, from where both Aunt Bessie and my mother had graduated, she started to take courses at Columbia for a Master of Library Science degree. So I frequently saw her at lunch time. When I was writing my freshman English term paper, she helped me a lot by critiquing it. It was about a Renaissance printer, Aldus Manutius, whom I found very fascinating. My research, for my satisfaction, for all such projects had to be absolutely thorough. I got an A+, no doubt due to Aunt Bessie's help.

Aunt Bessie attended many of the Chapel Choir's daily noon services, that I belonged to. We held services not only on Sunday, but short ones, including one anthem, at noon every weekday. She enjoyed hearing us sing. We were very good. One time she called my attention to the fact that when singing I often swayed back and forth to the music. I stood at the front end of the altos and so was very visible. Thereafter I tried not to sway.

Unfortunately, depression and the great fatigue Aunt Bessie was prone to got her again after one and a half years and she had to drop out of the Master's program. I missed her terribly and I depended on her emotionally. When I was cramming for exams at the end of my second year, I became depressed. I traveled to her apartment instead of going home. She went out,

I know, to call my mother (she had no phone). I stayed overnight. The next day she went back to college with me and sat with me in the park while I studied. She was very helpful, and I did okay on my exams.

A few years later, her doctor diagnosed breast cancer, and she had a mastectomy, the same fall my mother had her first surgery for colon cancer. Aunt Bessie had, at that time, some metastases to axillary lymph nodes. She had trouble with the wound not healing well, and her doctor, whom she loved, hurt her feelings by saying she must not be cooperating well. Some time later I added it all up: the pasty skin, depression, fatigue, overweight, and slow wound healing, and realized she must have been hypothyroid all her adult life, which her doctor never picked up. At that time other breast cancer treatment was not done. Two years later she developed metastases in her liver and had to give up her job (she had greatly looked forward to retirement). She came home to our house to die. She used the room that had for the most part been mine and slept in my bed.

It was over the Thanksgiving holiday and I stayed with her a lot, but I regret not talking with her about death. She didn't realize she was dying, and I realized later that she needed that conversation. She thought she had hepatitis. She said she felt frustrated because she wasn't getting well fast enough. A few days later she died in my bed. As on other occasions, I froze and had almost no feelings of grief. She was buried in the Chatham Fairmount Cemetery where her parents were buried. I had to go back to medical school for classes and didn't attend her funeral.

There have been eight breast cancers in our family, five of which resulted in death: Aunt Muriel (two); Aunt Bessie; Aunt Gladys; Aunt Olive; Janet Downs McCain (Uncle Fletcher's younger daughter); Frances, my sister (in 1992, she had a mastectomy and recovered and is a "survivor"); and myself (in 2000, see my chapters on "Retirement" and "Full Circle"—so far, I'm a survivor too). Other cancers, all of which seem to be genetically related to breast, were my cousin Bill (prostate), my cousin Louise and Auntie Nan (ovarian), and my mother (colon). My cousin Ted had lung cancer, but that's not related to the others as far as is known now. He was a lifelong smoker, the only smoker in our family.

Aunt Bessie was my primary source of support throughout my life up until I was in med school. That being the case, I wonder about my not attending her funeral and my lack of grief. There must be some explanation. I'll expand on this in my chapter on depression.

THE DOWN, OUT, AND DYING

NUMEROUS RELATIVES (AND TWO NON-RELATIVES) CAME HOME TO DIE OR TO STAY a time because they were down and out. There were some others before I was born; I have no details.

Aunt Muriel brought in a male friend who had no place to live. I was a very little girl. I wish I knew more details; it must have been an interesting story. He was asked to leave after some valuables were discovered missing.

My mother's mother (Grandma Downs) had lived with my Aunt Bessie in their Westchester County apartment. I knew she and Aunt Bessie had both been performing pianists and that there was no piano in the apartment. So I never heard either of them play. Grandma's favorite piece of music was Beethoven's *Moonlight Sonata*, and I tried to learn it, not very successfully. When we visited them there, she always gave me a very wet kiss, and I always felt uncomfortable with her. To compensate, the visit was a chance to be with Aunt Bessie. Grandma was an overweight, gray-haired woman who was always smiling. She had a peculiar habit of frequently blowing at her right shoulder, then the left. I wondered if she'd had a dandruff problem in younger years, but there was no evidence that I could see.

When I was about twelve, she had a stroke and needed some supervision, which Aunt Bessie couldn't give her because of her full-time job, so Grandma came to stay at the Homestead. My mother cared for her. She mostly stayed in her room, the "guest room," the one over my parents' dining room. However, she could easily hear me practice the piano down in the dining room. While she was still able to laboriously come downstairs, she came a few times to oversee my practice. I resented this and regret that I did, because I could have learned a lot from her. I felt that she was interfering with my piano teacher's prerogative. I asked my mother if I could stop the lessons because of this and she agreed, though I wish she hadn't. I was not much of a pianist anyway and she may have thought, *What the heck* (though in reality she would never have said that). She phoned the teacher, and I never saw Mrs. Smith again, which I also regret.

Grandma had another stroke and thereafter stayed confined to her bed, and she died at age eighty-seven. While Mom and Aunt Bessie were fixing her body upstairs, I played the first movement (the slow one) of the *Moonlight Sonata* downstairs. I'm sure Mom and Aunt Bessie heard it, but they said nothing. She was buried in the Chatham Cemetery, on the hill above our house, where her husband (whom I had never known) was buried and, years later, where Aunt Bessie and Aunt Sallie were also buried. I didn't grieve much.

The next to die was my Grandma Moore, when I was home from college (see "Those Grandparents").

My great-aunt Sallie, Grandma Downs' sister, who had for years played a large role in our family, was the next. She was unmarried, a fantastically witty talker, and I loved her. She was present at all holiday dinners and kept us all regaled with her stories. She was also an incredibly fast typist and did court stenography during her working life. It was said by my mother that she should have married her lawyer boss, but he was Jewish and she a devoted Episcopalian. She also loved our Episcopal minister, Dr. Shipler (see "Spiritual Autobiography") and did a great deal at St. Paul's Church, taking care of the altar cloths, accessories, and the minister's robes. She also had a stroke while I was in college, was bedridden first in the little room over Mom's kitchen, and later in my grandparents' master bedroom, though my mother cared for her. When she died, I felt I was inured to death, and though I had loved her, I didn't grieve. She was also buried in Chatham Cemetery.

Also, while I was a freshman in college, I had a friend who was a senior who had mental health problems, and for the summer following her graduation that year, I asked my parents to take her in while she adjusted to her new job. (See more about this in the chapter on Barnard College.) They readily agreed; it was part of being in our family to take in people.

My father's older brother Ledlie lived in Massachusetts with his wife, Aunt Mary, and their two children, Louise who was seven or eight years older than I, and Frank, who was four years older than I. Uncle Ledlie died of peritonitis after an appendectomy, and some months after that the family lost their home. So the three of them came to our house to live until they got back on track. Louise worked in the Flower Shop. Aunt Mary was a naturalist, who with Uncle Ledlie had run a camp for boys in New England. She told me a lot about nature lore and boy lore. One time during her first year at our house she learned that some neighborhood boys were setting fires in the woods down by the barn, near the greenhouses. She went there and literally took them over, teaching them camp lore and allowing fire to be used appropriately. The boys took to her and thought of her as a scout leader. She also was Fran's advisor for her Girl Scout nature badge.

Louise and Aunt Mary had very severe asthma, for which at that time there was minimal effective treatment. After a time they pretty much stayed in their room, the lower well room or den, especially Aunt Mary, with the doors closed, smoking marijuana, which provided a little relief. They were able to do very little, and Auntie Nan cared for all three. I loved that family and visited them in the den from time to time.

Frank, at that time, played the piano in the den. He used the third floor room, which had been Aunt Muriel's personal studio, for his bedroom. He was around a lot, and my sister and I practiced flirting with him, and we laughed and laughed. He loved music and had a gift for it.

They went back to Massachusetts after a while, but Aunt Mary got so sick she was bedridden and came back to our house to be cared for by Auntie Nan. This time she had a room on our end of the house (our parents used the corner guest bedroom then) and I visited her often. She assumed it was all asthma. She refused to see a doctor, and when close to death went back to Massachusetts to die. We learned from her autopsy (Fran thinks it was found while she was still at our house) that she had active tuberculosis and that's what killed her. We didn't attend her funeral, but for her I grieved.

Later, my tuberculin test was found to be very positive, but my chest was always clear. If that were to happen now, I would have been treated with antibiotics, but not then. Fran's tuberculin was negative.

Frank soon came back to our house because he was supposed to be attending Rutgers. This time he was very depressed: no laughter. Of course he was grieving for his parents, but later I realized in retrospect that he had mild manic-depression. If only there had been antidepressants then! He had a terrible time getting up in the morning, and the whole family thought about creative ways to get him going. My father finally put the alarm clock in a metal bucket so it could resonate and echo and placed it in the hallway outside his room. Even that didn't work and Frank missed so many days at Rutgers that he ultimately dropped out.

Some time later he returned to Massachusetts to live with and support Louise, who was by then too disabled by asthma to work, by working at Raytheon. Frank later, after Louise married, had one engagement and two marriages, all of which ended sadly. He had three children. In 2001, after a career in music publishing and composing, he died of ALS (Lou Gehrig's disease) after a slow decline. I attended his funeral, which was arranged by his children and was very poignant. His body was given to medical science. I grieved for Frank. Louise and Hal, her husband, had five children. They moved to California after having three or four of them because of her asthma. She did much, much better there, lived a long active life, and died in 1995 of ovarian cancer.

My "So-Called" Handicap

In the community hospital, Overlook, where I was born, the custom then was to keep mother and baby in for ten days. The baby was brought to the mother regularly to breastfeed. I was brought wrapped in swaddling clothes, and my mother did not think to check the rest of my body. At the last feeding before discharge, I was brought with the blankets askew, so my foot (or feet) were exposed. My mother, when she told me this, said she thought the nurse loosened the blanket on purpose. She was shocked to see that my feet were just little knobs on the insides of the ankles. She didn't tell me what the shock felt like to her, but I imagine she must have been very distraught. She discontinued breastfeeding then; I imagine her milk dried up.

When the family found out about my feet, there was a major gathering of ideas and wishes. On my father's side there was a distant cousin who was a doctor and he referred them to Dr. Barnett, who was Medical Director of the Hospital for Crippled Children, an orthopedic hospital in New York City. Arrangements were made, and at six weeks of age my mother carried me to meet Dr. Barnett. Dr. Barnett diagnosed club feet, a not very common deformity, but there was a standard course of treatments, and plans were made.

I say "so-called" because in the long run, the feet didn't handicap me nearly as much as the psychological consequences, which, added to other factors in my upbringing, did.

Dr. Barnett was a gray-haired, smiling, grandfather-like man, kind and gentle. For the first two years, this trip was repeated weekly, at which times the week-old casts were cut off and new casts were applied to my lower legs to try to force the feet into proper position. My mother thought this must have been painful and was why I cried so much.

As I grew, I got to know Dr. Barnett very well and loved him. The hospital waiting room was large, impersonal, and dark. We had to wait there for my name to be shouted out. But instead of going into examining cubicles, we were taken directly to Dr. Barnett's domain, the casting room. I remember him cutting off the casts and gently testing my feet for strength.

I learned to walk in the casts at nine months. The casts added strength to my legs, causing me to be able to walk early. On the other hand, they caused my lower legs to not grow normal musculature. Consequently, my lower legs have always been skinny and atrophied, a frequent embarrassment.

At the end of two years, it was deemed that I should have the first surgery, standard treatment. They cut the Achilles' tendons to loosen the feet, so I have scars down the backs of my ankles. I don't remember anything about the surgery then but it must have been awful. I was alone in the hospital for a week. My parents didn't visit because of the distance, and of course my ankles were in pain. I didn't see Dr. Barnett at all. I had ether anesthesia, with the face mask. What I do know is that by the time of the second surgery two years later, the pounding sound of the anesthesia machine caused me to react as if hypnotized whenever I heard a similar pounding sound. This reaction lasted until I was well into adulthood, when I realized the connection.

Between the two surgeries, I'm not sure if the casts were continued. I do remember the second hospitalization at age four. They redid the same cuts. I was constantly scared to death. The circumstances were the same except I think my Aunt Bessie visited once. The baby in the next bed dropped and broke her bottle of milk all over the floor. I knew I should ring for the nurse (whom I rarely saw), but didn't have courage to do so. When someone ultimately came and saw the broken bottle, I finally felt relief from my conscience.

Either then or after the first surgery, the casts were stopped and I went with both parents regularly to the shoemaker in the next town, Madison. He traced the outlines of both feet onto paper, then measured around each foot in several directions. The high shoes he made for me also had lifts in them to encourage proper positioning. I wore high shoes like that until I was fourteen and was always self-conscious about them, such as on my first day in kindergarten. When we came into the kindergarten, while my mother and the teacher talked, a certain little girl (who took ballet and always held her hands effeminately), whose name I remember well and who ultimately graduated from high school with me, stared continuously at my feet, and I felt humiliated and as if I could sink through the floor. This sense of humiliation, which was manifested by extreme shyness and a very soft voice, continued throughout school and college, especially in regard to boys.

Sometime after I learned to write, I wrote a letter to Dr. Barnett, really a thank you/love letter. Lo and behold he answered it with a beautiful letter that I have kept all the years since.

When I was entering third grade, Dr. Barnett recommended that for six months I wear a cast on my left leg, with the knee bent, so I had to use crutches. So I didn't attend school that term. I don't remember how my school work was tended to, but toward the end of that time I went to a fourth grade teacher, who was French, for French lessons after the school day was over.

In eighth grade, I played field hockey with the girls' team and did very well at it! Always before that I did poorly in gym, couldn't keep up, couldn't run fast, couldn't hit the ball, and was always chosen last. So I really enjoyed field hockey but I think it was hardest on my left foot. It started to pain me, and the second semester of ninth grade I was excused from gym. Mom and I went to the hospital. Unfortunately, Dr. Barnett had retired. I was devastated and grieved inwardly, but never talked about it. I was seen by residents in a cubicle. The residents never made eye contact with us. It was recommended that I have surgery on the left foot and it was planned for that summer. The call finally came in August.

That hospitalization was very memorable. Sedation didn't take, and I waited on a gurney for hours in the hall outside the OR, alone, wondering if they would do the correct foot. I felt increasing anxiety and didn't sleep until the ether was started. They cut a wedge from the side of my left ankle and fused the joint. I was in the hospital for four weeks, and in that time I barely said a word. My parents visited on Sundays, and Aunt Bessie on Saturdays. After the first week, with all the other girls in the large ward, I was gotten up daily into a wheelchair and taken to the roof to sit in the sun and do handcrafts. We were taken back to the floor for lunch and back up to the roof for the afternoon. No provision was made for toiletting, so I uncomfortably held my urine all day, until late afternoon when we returned to the floor and bed. Then I could use the bedpan. All that time I made no complaints or requests. When my period was due, I asked for a napkin, but the period never came, so I was embarrassed to have to give back the napkin. The nurse looked at me quizzically, but I could say nothing.

There was an elderly Irish man with an accordion who came to the floor Saturdays and played the same Irish songs over and over. It was a pleasant interlude. One patient I did make friends with was Rose Iacovino. She was a year or two younger than I, lived in Hoboken, and was in the hospital because she had been crippled by polio. The doctors felt surgery could strengthen her legs. We became close friends and later I visited her home, and we have kept up a good friendship until now, with occasional visits.

When I was finally discharged, I went by wheelchair to a back door where my parents had brought the panel delivery truck. At the door I was given crutches and was very annoyed, without showing it, at the nurse who held on to me too much. After getting home, my mother engaged a nurse, who had given her a lot of help with my Grandma Downs, to give me a bed bath! It was an interesting experience. Mrs. Williams was also the mother of the boy sitting in front of me in sixth grade. (See "Being a Loner: Public School.")

During that fall, I could walk in the cast, and a good friend, Gloria, who lived farther away from school and passed my house on her way, stopped in every afternoon with my homework. We became fast friends during that time. One course we both took was Spanish. At the end of the visit, sometimes in the evening, I'd accompany her up the hill to the corner of our street, and we sang Spanish songs in parts, standing on the corner. I also took stenography and typing. Gloria had a chronic cough (no doubt from the constant second-hand smoke in her home). One day my Aunt Muriel came into the dining room where we were sitting at the table, and to my embarrassment scolded Gloria because I was "sickly" and her cough was "bad" for me. Gloria took it good-naturedly and it didn't interrupt our work.

I didn't return to school until a few days before Christmas. I resented not being allowed to attend, especially after I found out that my friend Gertrude, having broken her leg and using crutches, was allowed to attend school. I'd expected to go in January, but my mother was insistent that I go as soon as I could walk okay.

When the cast came off and the crutches were not needed, I could walk very well. My mother and I went to a new shoemaker in New York to get my first shoes that were not high! When we went back to get them the next week, I was shocked and disappointed that the new ones *were* high, and to boot, made of a very fancy leather, probably very expensive, a kind of leopard design on a yellow base color. I was totally disheartened. I couldn't say anything, but my mother realized how I felt and that it was not what we ordered. She had the guts to refuse them and reordered what we wanted. I felt terrible, because the shoemaker had obviously put a lot of care into making a beautiful pair of shoes, but I couldn't have worn them. I wanted something that would look like regular shoes, not something so very obviously attention-getting. I still feel sadness for that shoemaker.

My mother was concerned because since the surgery, my left leg was shorter than the right. She was afraid it would tip my uterus and make childbearing hard or impossible. The resident measured from my hip bone to my ankle bone, and there was no difference. My mother felt foolish, I know. None of us—the resident, my mother, nor I—were observant enough to realize the difference in length was below the ankles! Years later I learned it would have no effect on pregnancy.

When I finally got the shoes I wanted, I returned to school feeling "normal." But for many years I continued to have them custom-made, until I was in my seventies and moved back to New Jersey. In med school, I had them made like dress shoes, so I would be comfortable and look good when working. My ankles became arthritic during adulthood, but by and large my feet did pretty well. In medical school I found a first-rate shoemaker who was able to make shoes that were fashionable. Later, after moving to Rochester, I went to New York for new shoes, and in the '80s and '90s to Toronto.

In the late 1980s, I asked a plastic surgeon friend if he could make the scar on the back of my left ankle less prominent. At the top end of it, the scar was deeply indented. He said he could. I went for one-day surgery at Genesee Hospital. I was given a local and listened the whole time to a tape of the *Trout Quintet*, by Schubert and was sorry that the surgery was over sooner than the *Quintet*. The scar was much improved. When I moved back to New Jersey in 2000, I found an orthopedic shoe store that actually was able to fit me shoes from off the shelf and not nearly as expensive. Being retired, I no longer needed dress shoes, and these look somewhat orthopedic, but they are extremely comfortable. I still hesitate (or refuse) to go to a beach without shoes and socks on because of my self-consciousness.

MUSIC, MY SOLACE

WHEN I WAS FIRST HOME FROM THE HOSPITAL AFTER BIRTH AND ESPECIALLY AFTER
the casts were put on at six weeks, I cried a lot, my mother said. She thought
the casts on my feet and legs caused pressure and pain. The orchestra that
my father founded would practice in the atrium (our living room). My
mother would place me in the carriage in the front hall, right next to the
atrium. The music appeared to soothe me. More than that, I really imprint-
ed on the music. I integrated it so much that to this day I recognize in my
heart the pieces that orchestra played. Music is my "transitional object," like
a teddy bear or blankey. I remember the *Sorcerer's Apprentice*, the *Overture
to the Bartered Bride*, von Weber's *Invitation to the Dance*, *Finlandia*, the
Oberon Overture, the *Coppelia Ballet*, the *Semiramidi Overture*, the
Rosamunda Overture, and especially the *Unfinished Symphony* by Schubert.
This symphony became a symbol of my father to me, because he never finished growing.

In my pre-school years, I continued listening. I remember a concert
they played in the school auditorium of some of those same pieces. For a little time, in elementary school, before the orchestra folded because of the
new music teacher at school (Mr. Collicotte), I played the drums and tym-
pani when they rehearsed.

Observing my interest, at age four my parents suggested that I take piano
lessons. I was very eager to do that. And so I started with Mrs. Smith, who
lived a ways down the street, on the way to the school. I loved the lessons at
first, but I didn't like to practice. However, I stuck it out until age twelve.
For a few years Mrs. Smith held annual recitals, but she was getting older and
couldn't keep it up. I never became comfortable playing before people, even
just one. I was impressed by Mrs. Smith's stories about the lives of the "great
composers." Some time during the elementary years, I remember announc-
ing to my mother that when I grew up I was going to be a "great composer." Sometimes I dabbled at the piano, composing chords and melodies.

My interest in playing piano waned, but our family started listening on the radio in the dining room to the Sunday afternoon broadcasts of the New York Philharmonic. I often listened while I sat at the dining table doing my homework or reading a book. My paternal aunts and grandparents often listened to their radio also. One time, when I was eight or so, I was passing through their music room on my way up to my room. They were listening to "The Swan" from Saint-Saens' *Carnival of the Animals*. I hadn't heard it before. It was so beautiful I stopped to listen to it all. And then, before I went on, I told Auntie Nan I was going to have that played at my wedding! (But I didn't.)

I also took three or four violin lessons, in a group under Mr. Collicotte, in fourth grade. That was dismal. I was much too shy to do that. He also came to our class weekly for singing and our teacher had to rehearse us other days. One time she came around the classroom listening closely to us. I figured she wanted to know if we were really singing, so I sang as loud as I could. But she was trying to choose someone for a performance in a later school play. She didn't choose me. I would not have been able to do that.

In junior high I joined the chorus, which rehearsed during lunch hour. That I loved because I didn't have to stand out, and I continued that all through high school. We gave some unmemorable concerts. I also joined our miniscule church choir, which was directed by Mrs. Alliebelle Woodward, the organist. There were just enough voices that I didn't stand out. Also, in high school during my last two years, I took voice lessons from Alliebelle (who also was employed at the flower shop by my dad). She said I sang slow songs much better than fast ones, such as "Habanera" from Carmen. The slow ones were more full of emotion, like "Ave Maria" or Mozart's "Alleluia."

Once I was invited by a friend to sing "Always" at her wedding, without her hearing me first. That was a disaster. I had terrible stage fright and didn't sound out at all. I also "played" the piano in the high school orchestra. That was also disastrous. The conductor couldn't even hear me. I did not gain any favor from him.

In high school, Fran and I listened to the "Hit Parade" on Saturday nights and were adolescent enough to enjoy it. Also during my teenage years, we somehow acquired an old-fashioned wind-up Victrola and one record that could be played on it, "The Beautiful Blue Danube Waltz." I loved it. Every afternoon after school, for a long time, I wound it up and played it over and over in the atrium and danced actively, whirling around. No one was there to watch me, and I felt free to dance as I wanted.

Once, in either junior or senior high, I tried to audition for a piano performance at school. I chose my favorite piece, "The Butterfly." I knew it very well, but I blew it after the first phrase and couldn't continue. I ran out through the auditorium, very conscious of listening teachers' stares. It was one of the most humiliating events in my life.

After graduation, I had a Philharmonic subscription with Aunt Bessie for a year. See her chapter ("My Confidante") for more.

When I started in college, I auditioned for the Chapel Choir (apparently my stage fright didn't bother the director) and, joyfully, got in. Then began four wonderful years of *a capella* choral singing under Dr. Lowell P. Beveridge. I loved to hear him play the organ. I learned a lot about sacred music from all the eras, starting with Renaissance. I made my best friends in choir, and after Sunday services, we often gathered in Riverside Park and sang. I also remember an occasion for which we went somewhere on the subway, and we sang our favorite anthems there, on the subway train, among ordinary riders. We stood together at one end of a subway car.

I early on learned that New York had a "good music" station, WQXR. I asked for and received a radio for Christmas, and thereafter had it on whenever I was in my room. I listened while doing homework until 1:00 A.M. when they played the theme music, *Rhapsody on a Theme of Paganini* by Rachmaninoff, when signing off. I took a music appreciation course, in which I wrote a fun (and well-graded) paper comparing the Berlioz, Mozart, and Brahms *Requiems*. Then I took a theory course, in which I did not do well. I went to ask the teacher how I could improve my grade. She thought I wanted her to change my grade and scolded me harshly. Even though she was wrong, I hurriedly left her office feeling totally disgraced. I'm sure she took that to mean she was right.

While at Barnard, I was also able to go to wonderful concerts at the University theater, which was right across Broadway from my dorm. I had free admissions by being an usher. I was in charge of the whole balcony. I remember one woman patron who didn't want me to show her to her seat because she had been coming for many years to the same seat.

I took a course at Columbia, across Broadway, on Renaissance music, and then one on conducting. In that I gained some self-confidence as the class was very small. And the choir did some special sing-alongs. In one I sang the alto in a lovely three-part song from Mendelssohn's *Elijah*, "Lift Thine Eyes." I actually did it! Once I even took an opportunity to conduct the choir with a piece I loved, "Come Holy Ghost" by William Byrd. I felt I did it well, but I was told I took it too slowly. Several other choir members also tried it that day.

One of my choir friends introduced me to live opera. It was too expensive for regular attendance, but again I learned a lot. She loved Wagner in particular, and we saw *Tristan und Isolde*, with the Liebestod, which I already loved.

A group of us in the dorm, including Jane C., another choir friend, listened every Saturday at 6:00 to the NBC Symphony conducted by Arturo Toscanini, who generally took faster tempos than other conductors. Their last concert was Beethoven's *Ninth Symphony*, the *Choral*. We wondered if

Toscanini could do it all in the allotted hour even though it usually went well over the hour. He did! He finished it a few seconds before 7:00. I also remember hearing the *Ninth* after the Berlin Wall came down, when Leonard Bernstein conducted it in Berlin. It was truly inspirational. He substituted "Frei" (free) or "Freiheit" (freedom, I'm not sure which) for every "Freude" (joy). What a marvelous sound it was!

Jane was quite troubled. She was two years behind me at college. She was not able to finish and was hospitalized at Rockland State Hospital in Westchester County with serious schizophrenia. I visited her there twice. After she was discharged, she was still not really well. I wrote to her at her home address, but never heard back. I tried to write again a few times, but I lost track of her.

During my two years at Mount Holyoke, there was little music. I couldn't even pull in WQXR. During the next four years at medical school (in New York City), I got WQXR but did little else musically, except for the time with Martin (see below) but in the last year or so did join a community chorus that had previously been conducted by Robert Shaw. Under the current director, however, it was not much. I did make one friend there because we took the same bus. She and I have kept up with Christmas cards ever since.

In the summer before my junior year at medical school, I was an extern at Kings' Park State Hospital on Long Island. There I met a man, Martin, my age, who was doing a conscientious objector stint. The wonderful thing about this friendship was his gift of music, although I admired and agreed with his social and political ideas. He played the violin and expected that would be his profession (which it eventually was). In the fall, after I returned to school, we continued dating, always at a friend's apartment where he and three or four others played wonderful chamber music. I learned and loved a lot. In particular, I remember Schubert's *Quintet for Strings*, two violins, one viola, and two cellos. In December Martin moved away, but we kept up a correspondence (See "Cornell" chapter). Thereafter I chose chamber music whenever I could.

After med school, I moved to Rochester, New York. During my internship, there was little music. In March, I married, and we discovered WBFB, which Wally and I listened to each evening. After finishing one year of the internship, I quit medicine for a time and started a family. I could also pull in a Toronto good music station, although not consistently clearly. However, the big opportunity came several years later, when Rochester's own good music station, WXXI, came into being. Wally and I have been faithful members of it ever since, for thirty to forty years, until I retired and moved back to New Jersey, where I can again get WQXR very well.

In the late '70s, I discovered the SCMR, the "Society for Chamber Music in Rochester." I subscribed to their series of concerts every year until

I moved away, with Wally (husband) at first, then with Lou (friend). After that, on some of my return trips to Rochester, I've been able to attend one of those concerts.

During the years in Rochester, I went to many concerts. In the early years I was in the Unitarian Church choir, but had to drop out due to family pressures. In 1990 I was able to join again, and this time had another fabulous director, Ed Schell, and it became an important part of my life. I can't decide which director—he, or Dr. Beveridge—has been better.

When I was pregnant with my first child, I joined the Rochester Oratorio Society. We sang "Carmina Burana," by Carl Orff, which was new to me then. The baby inside me responded and jumped about while we were singing. I didn't like the director. He was quite short-tempered and the chorus was too large and unwieldy. I'd been spoiled. I dropped out after that concert, as the baby was about due anyway.

In the '60s and '70s the University of Rochester Music Department hosted summer series of sings, the Oratorio Reading Choir. We did a different large chorus each week. We were not preparing for concerts and did little "rehearsing." It was a great deal of fun.

In the 1970s I took two years of group piano lessons with Marge Johnson, the choir director at church at that time. I found that my skills (such as they had been, without real talent) did come back. I got so I could play before the rest of the group of seven or eight.

For about ten years I was part of an annual reunion of the Columbia Chapel choir, at which we renewed old ties and sang our hearts out. It was full of nostalgia and love. Dr. Beveridge later died, as did his wife, and the reunions began to peter out. The last one was in 1998, I think. These are beautiful and favorite memories. John Jagy was the organizer, and I'm still in touch with him and his wife, Barbara, whom he met in the choir.

Shortly before retirement I got a hankering to compose again. Knowing I needed more music education to do that, I started taking theory courses in the community program of the Eastman School of Music, for two years before moving away. The next year I would have taken composition, but had to forego it. I did compose a few songs, mostly based on Robert Frost's and Emily Dickinson's poems. However, after moving, I began to lose interest. My computer program and electronic piano, bought for the purpose of making composing easier, didn't work well.

Since moving to New Jersey in 2000, I've continued to attend concerts, and several times returned to Rochester for a week, during which I sing in the church choir. Sometimes I can attend an RPO or SCMR concert. At home, I keep WQXR on all the time, setting it to go off after I'm asleep. In the morning it wakes me up. I am proud of and enjoy the fact that if I turn it on after the initial announcement of a piece, I can maybe 30 percent of the time identify the piece or at least the composer after a few bars of music, sometimes with the first note or two that I hear, especially music of the romantic and contemporary eras.

On a recent Rochester trip, I attended a Sunday matinee by the RPO, conducted by Jeff Tyzik, of World War II songs. They included many of my favorites from then: "The White Cliffs of Dover," "Praise the Lord and Pass the Ammunition," "When the Lights Come on Again All over the World," that Fran and I had listened to on the "Hit Parade." At the Senior Center that I go to now, an old radio plays those songs from high school that I remember so well.

The Unitarian Society that I attend now does not have a choir—never got going in spite of efforts, I've been told. I auditioned for one chorus that uses the church for rehearsals and an annual concert, but didn't like the director. There are other community choruses, and I may audition for one of them next fall. I'm spoiled by my past directors.

When I die, I want memorial services in both Rochester and East Brunswick Unitarian churches, and I want the Rochester Unitarian Choir to sing excerpts from the Faure' and/or the Durufle' requiems.

Listening to classical music is a great comfort to me, just as it was when I was a baby in the carriage listening to my father's music in the atrium.

In Their Bosom

At the time of my birth, my parents were sleeping in the room next to the back-stairs and partly under the split-level attic. At first I was there too. At some point, my parents were finally given the use of the kitchen, dining room, and atrium on the first floor in the first part of the house. Some time in the first year, I was given the upper well room. Except for some interruptions (e.g. after my appendectomy I used the guest room and in high school, the tiny room over Mom's kitchen) that would be my bedroom until I was in medical school.

About the time of my first move to the upper well room, my parents took over the room at the other end of the Z-shaped closet. My mother told me that a small Christmas tree was put in my room, shortly after I learned to walk (in the casts). She said I was entranced by the decorations and lights.

In my second year, three months before my birthday, my sister was born. Soon she was also sleeping in my room. This must have been not long before or after my first surgery. I'm sure it didn't help my spirits any. When my sister learned to talk, she called me Mimi. It stuck, and to this day she and her family call me Mimi, or Mime, or Aunt Mimi.

This was of course the period when Mommy and I made our weekly train trips to the Hospital for Crippled Children (now the Hospital for Special Surgery), located then where the United Nations building now stands. I only remember seeing my feet in a generally correct position. I don't remember seeing them as knobs on my ankles. Frances went with us and sometimes Daddy too, and we'd go to the Museum of Natural History after the hospital. After we were through with the casts, my mother, on doctor's recommendations, massaged my feet every night. This continued until I was in college.

At bedtime, while I got my feet massaged, Mommy and sometimes Daddy would tell us stories about when they were little. This kept up until we were in high school I think.

Mildred

Mildred and Shad

I remember going to Sunday School at St. Paul's Episcopal Church down town. After the school session, the regular service was held. I know my parents tried frequently to attend, and when they did, my sister and I would sit on the prayer cushions in front of them and draw pictures. I think we were pretty good at not making lots of noise. Our parents didn't always attend because of Daddy's business. Sunday morning was a popular time for people to have flowers delivered. I remember that after church when people gathered on the front steps to talk, ladies would say how "cunning" (cute) Frances and I were. I was the type, however, who hid behind Mommy's skirts. I knew my shoes were an object of attention. Later, when we were old enough to walk to church ourselves, my parents went less often.

When we were quite little, Daddy would take us and Mommy to Whippany Pond, quite a long ways away. Chatham didn't have a play-gound/swimmimg pool yet. Mommy would sit in a chair on the shore, and Daddy would teach us to swim. I think we became pretty good at it. The pond got muddier over the years. After we started going to camp, we practiced swimming there instead.

From early on, we were visited every Sunday afternoon by Aunt Olive, Uncle Harry, and Billie, their little boy whose age was between mine and my sister's. They lived in Summit, just on the other side of the Passaic River, not far from Overlook Hospital. Uncle Harry and Grandpa always played chess while the ladies talked. Fran, Billie, and I played, usually outdoors if weather permitted. It was with Billie that we discovered the mica in the foundation pit. These visits continued until Grandpa's death. Then Uncle Harry could have played chess with Dad, but I don't recall if they did.

Once Frances and I were invited by Aunt Olive to stay over night at their house. We must have been four, five, six, or thereabouts. I suspect that our dressing and undressing was to be educational for Billie (and us). At dinner, we got into a hilarious food-throwing game; I threw onions and Billie threw beets onto the white tablecloth. Frances threw food too. Aunt Olive had quite a time dealing with us. At that visit Aunt Olive taught me to tie my shoelaces. She was quite surprised that I didn't know how yet.

The visit was reciprocated a few weeks later. About that I recall only that Billie was unhappy being away from home. Other than Billie, we never played with other children. My mother was very protective. Our other cousins, whom we saw from time to time, were considerably older than we were. They included Ted, Ledget (later George), Carolyn, and Betsy, children of Aunt Gladys and Uncle George, who lived around the corner from us and to whose house a back path from our drive went through our woods; and Louise and Frank, children of Uncle Ledlie and Aunt Mary. It wasn't until school that I encountered any children my age other than Frances and Billie, except for a distant cousin of Betsy's on her father's side, Nancy, who came to all-family activities at Betsy's house, such as Christmas parties.

One story I was told was that I was watching Daddy take apart a wrench. "What is this?"

"Part of a wrench."

"Is this part of a wrench?"

"Part of a wrench."

"What is this?"

"Part of a wrench."

"That's a funny way to say yes!"

At age four, several things happened. I had the second surgery, one of the ones I remember best; I started the piano lessons, at first a high point of my week; also started art lessons with Aunt Muriel; and Daddy taught me to play chess. At chess, he never "let me win;" he took me very seriously. He always won, except the last game before I went off to college. We were down to one king each, a stalemate!

There is one rather vague memory—Fran doesn't remember it at all, so we must have been very young—we all went into the stair room, where Grandpa's radio was, to listen to a speech by King George the Fifth of Great Britain. I don't remember what the occasion was, but the folks explained that he was a very important man and that it was pretty exciting to actually hear him on radio. I couldn't understand a word he said (between static and his English accent), but I knew it was something very important.

At one holiday dinner, Aunt Sallie was regaling us with her stories while cutting the pie. She cut mine first, much too small. I figured she wasn't really paying attention, but my eyes filled with tears. Aunt Bessie, who sat next to me, noticed and deftly exchanged her pie, which was regular size, for mine and whispered that Aunt Sallie's spatial vision wasn't good. That was typical of Aunt Bessie and one of the traits that endeared her to me.

One summer day the four of us (parents, Fran, me) were preparing to go visit friends of my parents a long ways away who were camping at their summer cabin on a beach. It was as though we were going camping too, packing all the essentials. At my insistence, my mother allowed me to carry a huge and heavy glass water bottle to put in the car. I put my arms around it, like a bear hug, and started walking through the dining room to the front door. Suddenly it slipped out of my arms and crashed to the floor, scattering glass and water all over, especially over the front of me. I screamed, and there was a big commotion. I was quickly gathered into the truck, and driven by my parents to the Emergency Room of the hospital in Summit. Still screaming, I suffered the ether mask being pushed on my face, as I could see that my mother was being forced out of that room. That just terrified me more; today they would have kept her with me. After I was etherized, picked over, stitched, and bandaged, we went home and did go on the trip. I couldn't go swimming, but I relished the attention I got. My mother told me when I was grown that she still felt terribly guilty about that episode. I still have some tiny scars on my wrists, neck, and upper lip.

Daddy and I spent a lot of time together because I accompanied him on most of his drives to obtain and deliver flowers. The panel delivery truck was our only car. Some of our drives, with me in the front passenger seat, were quite long. We traveled all over northern New Jersey. We were buddies.

My Companion and Co-Struggler

My favorite sister, my only sibling, was so much a part of my growing-up life, and even of my adult life, that she is woven into almost all of these chapters, but I want to give her special recognition, because she has been so vitally important to me so many times.

Even though as youngsters we squabbled and even fought a lot during the day, at night we were friends sharing the same bedroom. We talked a lot then, about everything. In my letters to my friend from camp, Tinker, I said we were not friends but enemies. Tinker wrote back that her sister, considerably older, was a good friend (they had to run their house together, as their mother was sick with cancer). This made me think about Fran, that maybe we should be friends. I believe that that's one reason I began in high school to be a little friendlier toward her. She had many more friends than I did, but worried about her popularity too. She was much more people-oriented than I, more practical, and more assertive in general. She was able to argue more effectively with Mom, especially regarding things where Mom was just not up-to-date. When distressed, she was able to let it be known and to stand up for herself more than I.

We both, as time went on, had emotional problems and still do. She was hospitalized also, briefly, as an adult, and had much psychotherapy. As adults, we have shared intimately our feelings about our parents and family members, positive and negative. A lot of it is contradictory, both in memories and feelings.

Frances went to secretarial school after high school, then to Maryville College (co-ed) which had rigid, Victorian boy-girl activities and rules, for two years. She tells me she broke ten rules the first year. She transferred to the College of General Studies at Columbia University, majoring in American Literature, and got her B.A. For a long time she wanted to be a writer. She was published and always has a book in progress (usually fiction and often relating metaphorically to our childhood and family). After marriage and four daughters, at thirty-nine she returned to Columbia to the School of Arts and got her Master of Fine Arts. She became a lecturer in English at CUNY (the City University of New York). For many years there she taught English as a second language to adult students from many foreign countries, developed curriculum, and wrote a textbook for it. She co-initiated an educational writing movement, W.A.C. (Writing Across the Curriculum) which became nationwide over her last five years there. She gave many presentations. She retired several years ago so she could write full-time. She's continued to consult in her field.

I feel very close to her, her husband Dave, their four daughters, and ten (three being step-grandsons) grandchildren.

I've sought help from Fran many times. Although there have been large gaps in our contacts, we've remained close. For this autobiography she's been invaluable as photograph and old letter provider, consultant, commentator, informant, and editor.

Mildred — age 7, and Frances

Being a Loner

I think I must have started kindergarten in the middle of the year, because the class was going strong when Mommy and I walked in. It must have been after I recovered from surgery and right after my fifth birthday, in February. With Mommy's and Aunt Bessie's encouragement, I had really looked forward to school. However, that's when the reality of my strange shoes hit me, as they attracted stares from other children. My shyness was already established, but this new experience with other children was very scary.

I hated kindergarten. The teacher was mean and strict. My one solace was the assistant teacher. My mother asked her to supervise my toileting as I wasn't quite independent yet. This teacher was Miss Terhune, but I thought her name was Mr. Hune, and I was always confused about her gender.

An example of my shyness and non-assertiveness occurred one time when the class was standing in a large circle. I had to go to the bathroom, but I couldn't bring myself to get excused from the circle and I went right there on the floor. Of course this was far more embarrassing. The teacher scolded me in front of everybody. Fortunately Mr. Hune took me over and defused the situation for me.

First grade was better. The teacher, Mrs. Arrowsmith, was gentle and kind. I stayed close to her when we went outside for recess.

Second grade was eventful. I was having trouble learning to read and someone realized that my vision was impaired. I was taken to see an eye, ear, nose, and throat doctor, the same doctor who took care of Auntie Nan's sinuses. For the exam, he put drops in my eyes to dilate them, and he diagnosed astigmatism. In those days the drops were always long-lasting, so my mother wrote a note to the teacher saying I wouldn't be able to see the blackboard for a day. But the teacher didn't take it in. She called on me to read something on the blackboard. It was, to me, a total blank, and I muttered

57

something. The teacher scolded me, and I said no more. That teacher went down a notch in my estimation.

When I got the glasses, they were bifocals which I had to wear all the time. However, I could see print and blackboards much better.

One day I was reading aloud to the class, and I came to the word "nowhere." I couldn't get it; finally I said "now here." The class laughed and the teacher did too. After she corrected me I had an even harder time trying to read aloud, and she went down another notch. I felt utterly humiliated.

Also that year (it must have been summertime) because I'd had a series of Strep infections, it was decided that I should have a T&A (tonsillectomy and adenoidectomy). In those days, preventive surgery was often done, so Frances and Billie as well as I were hospitalized at Overlook. All three of us had the surgery. Billie was terribly upset about it. It was his second time away from home overnight (the first having been the overnight with us; see "In Their Bosom"). I felt smug because I had experienced hospitalization. For our "last meal" the night before, I was served a salad which had very visible pepper sprinkled on it. I couldn't eat it, and the nurse scolded me. But we enjoyed the ice cream after the surgery.

At home, my sister and I often squabbled and it often became physical. One time I had her arms grabbed in my hands and I was kicking her shins. My mother took me aside and said I had to be especially careful not to hurt people that way because my heavy shoes could hurt more than regular ones. This really impressed me, that I was especially strong and had to avoid hurting people because of it. This idea became fixed in my unconscious and added to my non-assertiveness.

In the barn down the hill lived a stray female cat. My mother fed her when she wandered to the house. After a time, lo and behold, she brought to our kitchen four kittens, one at a time. So then they were ours. Fran and I named all of them. Most of them we didn't have for long, but a male, black and white in patches, lived with us for many years. He was named by Fran and me "Billie Cat Moore," after our cousin (Bill's actual surname is Bustin). He was a real tomcat, never neutered in those days. He fought others, and at night in the spring I heard him from my bedroom, yowling from atop a fence. One time he experienced a very torn ear.

Another sound I heard in the middle of every night, often waking me briefly, was the chug-chug and whistle of a train in the distance trying to get up a hill, sliding back, and trying again, over and over. The identical chord as that whistle I much later found in one of our choir anthems. I also heard, especially in the summer, the strange call of the mourning doves. They always sound as if they are far away.

Frances had a friend named Bobby Simonson. One Saturday, he came over to play, and Fran wasn't home. I said I'd play with him. We threw a ball back and forth. I was on our back porch (outside Mom's kitchen) and he was on the ground below. After a while he asked to change places, which we did. As we passed each other, he whispered to me, "I love you." I was thrilled and tried to be even nicer to him. This was the first time I had a good experience with a boy. (Billie was "just a playmate.")

Our neighbors for a year or two took in a foster son, Jimmy, two to three years older than me, who was mildly retarded. Fran and I played with him often. It was he who was with us the time we saw Grandpa fall off the path.

One time my mother became very angry at me (why I don't know) and came after me, obviously ready to beat me. I ran screaming into the dining room and got under the table. She couldn't reach me, and after some scrambling by both of us back and forth under and around the table, she gave up and went back to the kitchen. I'm sure this wasn't the only time she got that mad at me, but it definitely stuck in my memory. I had a temper that flared from time to time, and my mother tried valiantly to help me learn to control it. My guess is she and I fed each other into it. Most of the time both parents— especially Dad—favored me over Fran in many ways.

One summer, the four of us took Grandma Downs to Saranac in the Adirondacks to visit her cousin Claude Downs, who was there because he had tuberculosis. It took two days to get there, and we camped overnight in a cow field. On one side of the truck was a window, a table with butter for breakfast on it, and an awning. While Grandma was inside doing her ablutions in the morning, she looked up out the window and saw a cow right there staring at her! She was completely flustered. The cow was mainly interested in the butter. This story was told many times.

Third grade was the year I had a heavy cast up to the top of my left thigh and missed school for a semester. I remember becoming quite skillful with my crutches, especially going up and down stairs. Fourth grade was relatively uneventful. I continued to have great difficulty speaking aloud in class and having no friends to speak of.

In Sunday School, I had the same teacher, Jeannie Johns, for several years. She was a short, chubby person who bubbled over with delight. I loved her and had quite a crush. She got married, which was very exciting to me. I didn't attend her wedding, but I took a wedding gift to her home. She moved away after that, and I greatly missed her.

At home, Daddy cracked many corny jokes over and over. Also, the massaging of my feet by my mother continued throughout the school years.

When the weather was good, after school I would wander the grounds. A favorite spot was "Moore's Rock," which jutted out from a slight hill between the newer part of the house and the street. Another was the stone wall running the entire length of the house next to the sidewalk. It provided good climbing exercise. Another was that woodsy little hill between the stone wall and Moore's Rock. Another was behind the house, a little steep path running down from the first twist of the driveway to near the top of the real path leading down to the greenhouses. At the top of this little path was an arbor I liked to stand in to survey the view. In winter this tiny hill was one Fran and I skied down when we were both given child's skis for Christmas.

I was given a tiny plot of land just outside our kitchen porch to grow plants. Gourds were chosen for me because they thrive regardless of care. They did grow well, and I did care for and watch them. I picked a couple for various purposes, but left the rest to grow into a mess. I never took to gardening or flowers for that matter. My father never called me into the flower business, nor Frances either, as his father had done to him. But I like to send flowers as thank-yous to friends.

I daydreamed a lot. When little, I had a make-believe girlfriend named Betty with whom I was always arguing. Her main role was to carry out the arguments I didn't have the nerve to carry out in reality. Later, I'd sit on the front porch step and dream an ongoing life with a boyfriend named Peter, who was kind, thoughtful, and wouldn't take advantage of me sexually or otherwise. This dream story continued until college.

After fourth grade, I went to a YMCA camp for two weeks. I was quite withdrawn but kept up with activities and enjoyed the structure. It was not a bad experience. Fran went to a Camp Salvador (at age seven) and was very homesick. The following year we both went to the YMCA camp and had wonderful experiences. After we got home, we tried to keep up the same structure as at camp—ceremonies, activities, and singing at meals.

I had two mishaps at camp. I and a couple of others got ready for rowboating, but the rowboat escaped and went downstream along the shore. I ran through the lush grass to catch it and stepped into a yellow jackets' nest. What an uproar that created! They flew up at me, and as we were getting into the boat, fed furiously on my back. I was screaming. I wanted to jump into the water, which would have been good, but I was restrained by the others. I was rushed up to the nurse's office and spent a couple of days there on my stomach, covered with medicine on my poor back. However, recovery was uneventful.

The other mishap was in horseback riding. I loved to ride the horses. One time we were walking near some woods. Suddenly, something spooked my horse. He took off at a gallop through the woods and bushes. I hung onto his mane, lying down. The reins had escaped from my hands. That trip lasted a good five minutes or so. He calmed down on the other side of the woods, and I picked up the reins and walked him back. I was amazed that I had stayed on! I unfortunately don't remember what the counselor said.

When our folks arrived to take us home, they surprised us with a new puppy, a beautiful Irish setter that Aunt Bessie had given Mom. She was named Gypsy and was six weeks old. Fran remembers this meeting quite differently, that it was at home. Gypsy was lively and wiggly and love came immediately. She became a wonderful companion for my mother.

Two or three times during those years, Mom's brother, Uncle Fletcher, his wife, Aunt Jennie, and their two daughters, Edith and Janet (they were several years older than we were), came north from Baton Rouge, Louisiana, to visit us for several days. It was always exciting, especially the rearrangement of sleeping facilities. Sleeping on the floor on mattresses was prestigious. We took the guests to Asbury Park at the shore, where we went every summer, to swim. Janet got caught by an undertow too far out and was pulled way out beyond her depth. A lifeguard saw her and dashed out for her and got her back, unconscious and not breathing. He put her down on her stomach and did artificial respiration (in those days you pushed on the lungs from behind; CPR had not been developed). She finally, after letting quite a lot of water out of her mouth, came to and was saved. I hope that lifeguard got the thanks he deserved!

The next summer, 1939, when I was eleven, we went to the YMCA camp again. I did not do well; I believe I was depressed. Toward the end of the second week, the camp director asked me if I would like to stay another week. She apparently was going to call my mother. I really didn't want to and knew my parents couldn't afford it, but she talked me into staying. That third week was miserable. I remember an important event on September 1, the day before we went home: Hitler's invasion of Poland (I remembered it as being Czechoslovakia). It added to my depression, and when we went home I felt no better. It took a while for me to feel better enough to go back to school, but in fact school helped.

Every year through sixth grade my mother brought to class a Valentine birthday party for me. Sometimes it was a "surprise." She didn't want to leave anyone out by having a party at home. I enjoyed the food and attention but was embarrassed about it. One time (fifth or sixth?) the teacher sent a sealed note home by me a few days before my birthday. I couldn't resist the temptation and opened it carefully. It was about the party; I should wear a pretty dress, and it should be a surprise. Of course I felt terrible remorse and tried to put the note back together. I'm sure my mother realized what I had done, but never said anything. When the day came, nothing was said about my dress.

I had only a white blouse and a plaid skirt which I wore day after day for months it seems. It was the years of the Great Depression, and flowers being a luxury business, money was scarce. We always ate well, but I remember only once actually buying clothes with my mother. We did receive hand-me-downs from Aunt Gladys, who made them herself, and her two daughters, Betsy and Carolyn, who were four and eight years older than we were (her older children were sons, Ted, and George—known then as Ledget). I believed they were better off than we were because their father, Uncle George, "went to business," commuting to New York. But I didn't like to wear hand-me-downs. Uncle George died suddenly of a heart attack while Betsy and Carolyn were teens.

I enjoyed making things. One time I made a complete playground out of light cardboard. It took me weeks to finish. By the end, I was a little bored with it but made myself complete it. Another time I started to index the National Geographic, which I read regularly. I put a great deal of time and care into the project and was thoroughly disheartened when I learned they already published an Index. I quit the project then. Generally, I had to be thorough.

The main thing that happened in fifth grade was that the pediatrician called my mother and persuaded her that I should have a preventive appendectomy because I had sometimes complained of a stomach ache (not recently or currently though). I didn't take to the idea, because it would mean breaking a perfect attendance record at school. I rarely got sick and except for the first semester (in third grade) missed almost no school and was proud of it.

I was in the hospital ten days I believe. I was the only one in the children's ward, except for a five-year-old boy who had a badly infected thumb. The boy cried a great deal and several family members visited a lot and brought him oatmeal to eat. I thought he was terribly spoiled but now I would think more sympathetically of him. He was there only a few days, and then I was alone again. The fact that I was alone may bear on why they wanted to do the surgery—they needed to drum up business. Now, Overlook is a large and very very busy medical center.

I think I handled that episode fairly well, except for a few nights after the surgery. I suddenly, in my sleep, had the first post-surgical bowel movement, in my bed. I reluctantly rang for the nurse. Finally an attendant came and scolded me roundly and continuously while cleaning up. I couldn't say a word. Another time I had a bad leg cramp. This time the nurse was kind and helpful.

When the doctor took out the staples (not stitches), I was left with a thick, twisted scar in an abdomen also twisted. This didn't bother me until I married! Staples are no doubt designed differently now. Then it was a new thing.

When I returned home, I was told I would sleep in the corner guest bedroom right atop the back stairs. It was the one Aunt Bessie usually used when she visited. Some time before this, my sister had moved to the room next to the upper well room, leaving me with my own room, the other side of the Z-closet, and our parents had again taken over the one opposite the two-room bathroom (where they and I had lived when I was first born) and under the split-level attic (their ceiling was a little low). Recently, Fran had gotten the parents' room, so she and I had opposite ends of the Z-shaped closet when our parents had gone to the older room. I think Mom was worried because of the operation, and the end bedroom (or guest room) was closer to theirs than my regular room was. I remember she tucked me in at night especially carefully, but I recovered fine. I believe I used this room until Grandma Downs moved in with us after her stroke.

For Valentine's day, the class exchanged cards, and I got one! That was a surprise as I didn't have any friends in that class. I puzzled a while, figuring who might have sent it. Years later, I realized the teacher must have sent it, but then I finally decided it must have been the hyperactive boy sitting in front of me. He had trouble with his studies, but he said hello to me sometimes, and I decided to be nice to him. I never told anyone my thoughts.

One of the favorite sports among my schoolmates was ice skating on the "freshet," a wooded area that flooded and froze in winter. I went there once, but couldn't skate because my ankles weren't strong enough and my feet were too small to balance me. I never went again. I was always sad that I didn't have friends and blamed it on my shoes. Of course it was my shyness, I realized much later.

The walk home from school was up the hill, very tiring for me. One day, halfway home, a classmate's mother drove by, and I had the poor judgment to ask her for a ride. She reluctantly agreed, but was going downtown to shop. So I rode down, waited while she shopped, then rode home. I never did that again.

The one girlfriend I felt I had was in the other sixth grade. Her name was Gertrude. Every day I asked permission to go see her before the opening ceremony until my teacher got tired of my asking. Gert invited me to her birthday party (I think the only one I went to that wasn't for a relative), and I took her aside to tell her she was my best friend. She replied, graciously, that so-and-so was her best friend, but I was next. That felt good and lasted me for a long time.

INTRODUCTION TO SOCIAL SKILLS 101

In junior high (at that time seventh and eighth grade) I encountered a new world, one in which we changed rooms for different classes, had lockers in the hallways, had home rooms, and had to take responsibility for our schedules. It meant a lot more socializing in the hallways. I was just beginning to realize my responsibility in my own "lack of popularity." I took to reading many self-help articles in *American Girl* and *Seventeen*, and tried to act on them. It took a long, long time, and the residuals still remain.

We had four teachers, each one having a student-inspired nickname (not used to their faces!). There was Fuzzy-Wuzzy, Daisy, Hoagie, and Mattie. The best was Daisy (math). We respected her. I was often "teacher's pet." I continued to get almost all A's. I felt my classmates were beginning to respect me. I had never received harassment as a nerd, at least not to my face. Very gradually I started to make friendships in which I could talk a little.

I belonged to the Girl Scouts, who met at the Congregational Church across the street from our house, and I actively earned my badges. The one I remember best was identification of trees. In addition to writing about them, I went around town photographing them. I still recognize maple, oak, fern-leaf beech, cedar, pine, tulip and spruce.

I enjoyed the meetings and members. The summer after seventh grade I went for two weeks to a Girl Scout camp, a new one to me. I looked forward to it very much, but I had a terribly lonely time. At one of the first meals, I suggested we sing songs, as we had in my previous camp. I was reprimanded by our counselor at the table. This seemed to set my tone to the other girls in my tent.

In the middle of the two weeks, on Saturday, I came up the hill from swimming by myself, feeling very sad. Lo and behold, Aunt Bessie met me on the walk! I was so relieved I cried. She didn't drive, so I have no idea how she got there, but she listened to me and was very helpful. The rest of the two weeks was a little better. I returned there the following year and had a vastly different experience.

Eighth grade continued slightly better. I really enjoyed chorus and felt I belonged to that group. This was the year I played field hockey, from which my self-esteem gained a lot. It required little running, but mostly quick moves with the hockey stick, which I was good at.

It was December of that year that Pearl Harbor was attacked. I was in the dining room when the radio program was interrupted by the announcement. The next day, Monday, the whole high school and junior high were called into the auditorium to hear President Roosevelt declare war against Japan. My class sat in the balcony in the farthest section from the radio. I couldn't hear it, but I got the message. Back in class, we didn't discuss it.

I received a DAR citizenship award at the eighth grade graduation. (I never figured what deed of mine that was based upon!) This was also the year I stopped the piano lessons, and Dad taught me algebra.

One fall I helped Dad deliver telephone books. He paid me a portion of what he got. The distribution place was a chocolate warehouse. The odor there of chocolate was so strong it was not recognizable as chocolate. Unfortunately I was not turned off chocolate! I still love it. But if ever I smell that powerful stench, I know it will take me right back to the phone books.

An incident occurred that focused my attention on my need to know the truth. In art class we made portraits of classmates. My subject was a girl I knew. She had a scar on her forehead due to a bad auto accident she had had a year before, which had kept her out of school for many months. I put the scar in the portrait with minimal thought, only a belief in the truth. She demurred, rather softly and with a sad face, and I said, "But it's there." There followed a debate in my mind about the ethical dilemma, but I left the scar there. The portrait was posted on the wall with the others. I felt exposed and cruel, but still believed in the truth. A few days later I was badly criticized by another girl who had, she said, until then admired me a lot, but no longer. That dilemma has recurred many times. Only many years later did I realize how deep this issue was ingrained as a major part of my moral psyche, and that it had something to do with my career choice of medicine and then psychiatry.

The Girl Scout camp the following summer went very well. I was in the "top" tent, with the oldest girls and with a very good counselor, Terry. I made a friend in the next bed, Tinker, when I loaned her some clean sheets. Thereafter she and I were close friends. The year after that camp, she and I exchanged overnight visits. Her mother died from cancer that year. We still exchange Christmas letters, and now that I'm back in New Jersey we intend to see each other again. Our correspondence was broad. Tinker (Jane Tanner) dubbed menstruation "covered hedges," because she found a napkin on a bush.

One day at camp I found a little snake. I was sure it was a garter snake and picked it up the proper way (holding it behind its jaws). Others yelled at me to drop it and, startled, I did. As I released my hold, it peed on my hand. Others looked for it again to be sure of its identity. I was rushed to the nurse's station to be sure I wasn't bitten. I felt smug that I knew it was all unnecessary, but relished the attention. The nature counselor did find it and confirmed its being a garter snake. Then I was released from the nurse. I also passed the swimming tests that year at camp.

Back at home that summer I was invited by Aunt Gladys to go with her and Betsy (whom I admired) on a picnic outing. Unfortunately, that morning my first period started, and my mother encouraged me to decline the invitation, because of my self-consciousness. I regret I did, as I would have enjoyed it. My mother didn't believe in modern sanitary napkins. She had me wear diapers, which didn't help my social attitudes any. It was a year or so before I was bold enough to insist on using modern technology. I remember asking Fran if I needed a bra yet. She replied that I should have already gotten one, but I couldn't talk to Mom about it, and it was a long time before I got one, maybe when Fran ultimately did.

That summer, we learned that in the fall the neighbors across the street, Mr. and Mrs. Woods, would have two brothers and a sister come to stay with them from England for the duration of the war. Many families were doing this. I liked the Woods. They had a Scottie dog that I liked and played with. Their children were grown. I found out that the oldest English brother, Roddy, was my age and would be in my grade. Just as I began to fantasize becoming acquainted with him, I learned he was going to be sent to Bordentown, a military school. Before he left he did go to our school, my class, for a day or two. I admired his English accent from a distance.

The sister, Virginia, was aged between me and Fran and had red hair. She was a brash kid, but we did become friends. They stayed a few years. The summer and fall of my surgery year, she spent a lot of time at our house, playing cards mostly. We also formed a three-person club, with three officers (Fran, me, and her) and many rules. I think I must have been secretary, as I remember taking minutes then reading them.

The other brother, George, was six or seven. We didn't get to know him well. He had trouble adjusting to the changes and was a handful for Mrs. Woods. One time I babysat with him for an afternoon. He was a handful all right! I forget what he was playing with, but before I knew it he set the kitchen window curtain on fire. I was right there and was able to quickly put it out. However I wasn't asked to babysit him again.

At Christmas time, I became the bookkeeper in the flower shop, because I was good at numbers and organization. I did this every year until college. The flower shop was an exciting place at those times, and I enjoyed the challenge of keeping everything on track.

For two years, I cared for a large hutch of Flemish Giant rabbits in our back yard. They belonged to a friend of Dad's who was traveling. I fed them and cleaned the cages. One new rabbit was still immature, so I was flabbergasted when she produced a litter of babies. The babies died. Later, there was an epidemic among the rabbits, and they died. Their owner returned shortly after. I felt very apologetic, but he assured me I did nothing wrong.

In my freshman year, my left foot began to hurt (was this from playing field hockey so enthusiastically?) probably from arthritis due to the past surgery, and I was excused from gym. My friend Gloria was also excused due to her chronic cough, and we had a good time together. We weren't allowed to do homework during gym time. Some time then I began an afternoon job three days a week at the Chatham Public Library, shelving books. I learned a lot about the Dewey Decimal system and thus had that much more in common with Aunt Bessie. Involving numbers and alphabetizing, I was very good at that job. I continued it throughout high school.

I began thinking about my future. I was keeping a journal, and I wrote that my classmates were hopelessly uninterested in the big word "chemotherapy." That's what I wanted to do—to be of service, or therapeutic. The words sounded exciting.

Sophomore year was the one right after the big surgery. During that time, Aunt Bessie and Mom had a college friend visiting. This woman's niece was Ruth Webb, badly disabled. It was when I first heard of her. Later, she became very important to me ("Barnard" chapter). That fall was when Gloria came to my house daily with my homework. We took Spanish from an excellent teacher, who used music a lot. When I returned to school, with my new, relatively "normal" shoes, I was placed in a small advanced plane geometry class taught by Dr. Jeter, who was the high school principal. We all admired him greatly. The students in that class were welcoming to me, and I did very well. I was even able to solve a certain problem that we all worked on that even Dr. Jeter couldn't solve. That year, for a while, I slept in the tiny room over our kitchen, got a feathercut, felt much better about myself, stopped biting my fingernails, and started wearing lipstick and nail polish, in spite of Mom.

I got hold of a used bike and decided to learn to ride it. I walked it up to the corner above our house and got on to ride down a long hill away from home. It went down the hill all right, and I found its brakes didn't work! I should have continued to coast, as the hill flattened a long ways away. Instead I decided to stop it by riding into a curb on a side street. I did avoid hitting a tree, but I flew head first over the handle bars, landed on the sidewalk chest first. My glasses scooted across the walk, and I was knocked out of breath, but sustained no injuries. I walked the bike home, quite a walk up that hill. That was the end of that.

That year I developed a friendship with Dr. Jeter's daughter, Eleanor. The Jeters also lived farther up the hill and two or three blocks farther to the east. She also visited me a lot those months I was "laid up." I developed a real crush on her, the second of many (the first was on Jeanie Johns, my Sunday School teacher). Frances also became close friends with Eleanor. After I was in college, and Fran was struggling with the idea of college, Eleanor strongly advised her to go. Fran was more upset, and I wrote her a letter supporting what I thought was her real wish—to go to secretarial school. That exchange with Frances I date as the pivotal point at which we started being real friends instead of squabbling rivalrous siblings. Junior and senior years went even better. I still didn't have friends with whom I could "hang out," but I felt liked and respected by my classmates.

There was one boy I could talk to a little, Dana C. He was a year ahead of me, so he wasn't in any of my classes. He had hemiplegia (a weakened left leg and arm). He limped and his left arm was useless. He told me it was a result of a T&A operation that had complications. I felt a little safer with him because of his impairment. He also lived above on the hill, several blocks away, so he passed our house on his way to school. One day, he passed by the house and caught sight of me just leaving. He slowed his walk, but I didn't have the courage to catch up with him. Later when I got home my mother, who had watched from the window, told me I should have. I began to time my leaving so I could walk with him, and we became acquainted. I learned he played chess, so I gathered my nerve and invited him to come to my house to play chess. I did only fair with that. He later invited me to a movie and a soda afterward. I felt quite uneasy through it all. We didn't date again.

Field trips were infrequent. The one I remember best was the time our English class, under Miss Partridge, who was a very fine teacher of literature, went by train to New York to see Shakespeare's *Othello*. Paul Robeson (a Rutgers graduate and classmate of my dad) played the title role, Jose Ferrer was Iago, and Uta Hagen was Desdemona. They were all splendid, but I remember Robeson especially as being nothing short of fabulous. What a wonderful experience! Dad remembered him for being on the football team at Rutgers.

The summer after my junior year I took a summer "war job" to do my share in the war effort. Everyone I knew had a strong sense of patriotism. This was at the time when my dad was also working war jobs. I earned $18.75 per week. I was a filing clerk and "gofer" at Western Electric and developed a crush on a sexy girl named Billie, several years older than me. We kept up our friendship for several years. I also developed a crush on a young man there who was nice to me. I was greatly disillusioned when I noticed a pack of cigarettes in his shirt pocket. Also, I made friends with a machinist on a factory floor (very noisy), to whom I carried blueprints. He and I conversed a lot, shouting at each other over the machinery. On the train each day, I continued my ongoing daydream about Peter while looking out the window. There were thousands of locust trees growing alongside the tracks.

The following year, my senior year, was eventful. Doc Eschelman, a teacher of history and political science (PAD—Problems of American Democracy), was a favorite of all of us. We had very stimulating discussions. I still said little, but felt I was really participating and did well on papers, etc. We had a new Spanish teacher who, in her first post-college year, liked to talk to the girls about her upcoming wedding. She was a lousy teacher, giving us first-year material. I really missed the first Spanish teacher and learned little Spanish.

The only other boy I talked to was Bailey B., who was in my dance class (see below). We never dated. We did co-edit a literary magazine, "*The Round File*," and a couple of times we walked together to the printer's shop. I was able to talk a little. As "*The Round File*" was ready for printing, the weather was extremely hot and I had to announce at a full-school assembly that it would come out late because "the printer's rollers were melted." That brought a big laugh from the students, which pleased me.

Nineteen forty-five was a very special year, not only for me but for the world. I made an elaborate scrapbook about that year. FDR died and Truman became president; V-E Day occurred in the spring; and the atomic bombs and then V-J Day in the summer. It's hard to convey the very strong sense of patriotism we all felt during the war.

It was the year my father taught me to drive. We went to where there was an oblong circle, a street with a very wide median. We drove round and round that circle. When I took my exam, I had to drive up a steep hill, brake, then start up again. It was with manual transmission—automatic transmission was still a long ways off. I did it and passed the test. To help me socialize generally, I took dancing lessons for two years. I was clumsy and didn't do well, but I persevered. It turned out that Bailey was also in the dance class, and I got to dance with him sometimes. This was thrilling and anxiety-provoking for me. But he already had a girlfriend, Gertrude, my elementary school friend. In preparation for the dance finale I had to do something about shoes. The custom-made shoes were "normal," but not for dancing. I actually took two slipper soles and stitched crosspieces of green velvet across the top and actually wore them for the dance. I can't say they were successful, and I never wore them again, although I had spent a lot of time putting them together. In something like this my mother was not very resourceful. I did not attend the junior or senior prom.

I wanted to go to the dance class finale and tried asking one boy, who said, "No." My mother later told me she had met that boy's mother in the grocery store and that the mother said her son told her that in school I said little in class but that what I said was always important. I couldn't believe this and asked her for details. She rebuffed me and didn't want to answer me.

Years later I realized that many times she did lie to me, supposedly to help my self-esteem or, on the other hand, to promote my concerns about my feet.

My dad had an employee in the store who had two sons our ages. The adults conspired to make arrangements for both Fran and me (Fran doesn't believe she attended it, but I remember her doing so) for the dance. The boys brought corsages. The dance itself was not a highlight. Ever after that I've hated to dance, very self-conscious and unable to follow. Following meant putting my legs against the boy's, which I didn't realize to be one of my problems until I was an adult. I've always refused, but my husband persuaded me one time. It was terrible—I was all feet, stepping on his toes, etc., and in front of friends yet.

I applied to only one college, Barnard. I'd thought a lot about it and insisted to myself that I chose Barnard not because my mother and aunt went there and Mom's dad and Uncle Fletcher went to Columbia for engineering, but because of its very fine advantages. Even though I would take a year off, I applied anyway and dated the application a year ahead. The Admissions Office didn't notice this, and it resulted in some correspondence with them.

The High School Yearbook was very important. In mine, I got every member of the class to sign it. Many wrote nice things, including one, "Keep that great smile!" That was very gratifying to me. I was also voted "most likely to succeed." Throughout my school career, I sometimes felt like a "teacher's pet," though the teachers were rarely open about it.

I was selected to be valedictorian (in a class of seventy-six), so had to make a speech at the graduation. I chose a topic totally unlike any other valedictory speech, "Blood in War and Peace." No one told me it was inappropriate. The minister at the Congregational Church across the street from home, where I had been participating in some Scout and youth activities, volunteered to coach me. He took me to a basement hiding place in the church and had me take off my blouse and bra, explaining that he could monitor my breathing better. Then, sitting behind me, he fondled my breasts while he pretended to be coaching me. It was a very embarrassing experience. I didn't realize it was sexual abuse—which it certainly was—until years later. I never told anyone about the episode. To his small credit, he did offer me some pointers, and we talked about my stage fright, but that didn't undo the fact that he had molested me. He was discovered and fired when another girl did report him.

The graduation went off okay. We had no microphones then, and I managed to shout my speech, but I doubt the audience heard it, which was just as well. I kept my fists clenched around pink tissues. I also received a citizenship award, as I had at my eighth grade graduation. The diploma is stored somewhere in my leftover boxes.

The In-Between Year

By the time of high school graduation, I had decided to work for a year to earn money for college. The family was a little better off since Dad had taken the war jobs, but he was still the breadwinner for Grandma Moore and the two aunts, as well as my mother and sister, and at times others who lived with us for a time. I had been saving money since my preschool years. I had been influenced by "Uncle Don," of radio's child-friendly program. Later on we laughed at Uncle Don, but he did have this influence on this important behavior. But it wasn't enough. I was very idealistic and wanted to take responsibility for myself and take part in the war effort and pay for college.

During this next year at home, besides my job, I worked with my dad in the basement to make an elaborate wooden bookcase of my own design. It had a large bottom drawer that drafts could fit into and at the center was a small mirror over two note card-sized drawers. I used it in every home I've had until moving back to New Jersey, where I have less space.

Dad and I went to Madison weekly in the evening to take French lessons. His employee, Alliebelle Woodward, went with us. I had just learned to drive. In the winter, I was driving down a steep hill in Madison, lost control of the truck on the ice, and careened down the hill, hitting both curbs back and forth. Dad, who was sitting behind me, reached over my shoulder to take the wheel, but of course couldn't reach the brake. We eventually came to rest against a curb. There was, thankfully, no other traffic. He made me continue driving, else I might have lost my nerve.

The teacher of that class was very bigoted, as were other students, and talked deridingly about blacks, many of whom lived in Madison. Dad and I were very uncomfortable about this, but didn't say anything.

Also, I was feeling increasingly hostile to my mother and didn't want to sleep at home, at least partly because by then I hated the foot massaging. I swore to myself that I'd never sleep at home again. This, I believe, was adolescent rebellion. I found a job as night companion to an elderly woman living up the hill a ways near the cemetery. My father walked me up there every night at 10:00, and I spoke to her from her door. In the morning, I called goodbye to her and left. On one Saturday morning, I allowed myself to stay in bed later but was thinking a lot about how I was living my life. My job was dreadful and I was feeling there was so much I needed to do. I think this was a turning point in my attitude toward time. Thereafter, I tried not to waste any time. At that point, I got right up out of bed.

I applied for a job at Bell Laboratories and got one without difficulty. One of the departments was still in New York City but planned to move out to Murray Hill, not far from my home in Chatham. A major part of the company was located there already. Although I would start with a train commute to New York, I soon would have a very easy commute by special bus to Murray Hill.

This department mainly worked with crystals to be mounted in transistors and the like. The technician who did most of the mounting was a young woman who didn't want to move, and I was to take her place. That summer was memorable for continuous rain which was most noticeable on the ferry ride across the Hudson. That's where I was when news of the first atomic bomb was announced. I overheard some businessmen discuss it. It was horrifying.

The technician taught me the work, using heat and solder to mount wires on the quartz crystals, which were very sensitive to heat and broke easily. There was a subtle trick to making it work without breaking the crystal. At first I seemed to do okay, and in the fall the move was made. I still had some difficulty doing it, and many of my crystals broke. It seemed to be getting worse over the next weeks, and they trusted me with fewer crystals. I had less and less to do, so I hung around with the engineer who made machines and appliances for the department, and I did some reading on the topic of crystals and transistors. But I was quite depressed. Finally I broke a large, even more precious and expensive crystal, and I showed it remorsefully to the chairman. I was given no more. A few weeks later, in early December, the chairman told me they had been able to persuade the previous technician to move to the suburbs and work for them again, and I was being terminated. I would be welcomed back as an engineer after college, but that was little comfort. Actually I was very relieved to no longer need to feel useless and depressed. I was sent to the personnel office. They helped actively in finding another job for me.

I took a job in Newark as a secretary in the Prudential company. It would start in January. I was told I'd have to be able to take dictation, so for some days before and after Christmas I practiced my shorthand, my mother reading to me from *An Apartment in Athens*, a war novel. She didn't want to read a certain sexy paragraph, and I was annoyed with her.

At the new job, I was first given some accounting charts to do, and I did so well, I was never asked to take dictation. The office was fairly large, with a number of young women secretaries, who were not very welcoming. One girl, Jean, was pleasant, but I regressed to my extreme shyness. Here was the first place that I actually experienced ostracism. My lunch time was changed because a certain group did not want to eat with me.

A few weeks into the job, a new man was hired to a new office management job, named Allie (Albert) and he became friends with me. I suspect my introversion had something to do with their hiring him. I liked him, learned his life history, and developed a crush on him. He was married and had a young baby. My crush was not romantic. I was eager to meet his family. I began to spend lunch time writing in a journal, the first time I thought about autobiography. Allie continued to be very supportive of me. He called me "painfully shy."

In August, when I was readying to quit and go to college, they hired a girl just finishing college to take my place. She had been a math major but I gleaned that she had gotten by with a lot of cheating and had great difficulty learning the job. Allie told me that when I wasn't there one afternoon (I had gone for a pre-college interview), she had become hysterical. He tried to help her, but assured me I should not worry about leaving the job to her.

Jean persuaded the group to get me a going-away gift, a lovely sweater. It was placed on my desk with no comments. Knowing that most of them were really not in favor of it, I couldn't find the courage or way to thank them. Jean reprimanded me. Allie recognized my pain. I felt terrible. After I left, I did send them a thank you note. I was glad to get out of there and glad this year was over.

Later that fall, after a few weeks at college, Allie invited me to come to his house, presumably so I could meet his wife and baby. However, when I arrived, it turned out that wife and baby had secluded themselves from me, apparently thinking I was threatening. Allie didn't want to talk about it. It was a very strained visit. I kept up with him by Christmas cards and ultimately his wife accepted me as a friend. When he became ill a few years ago, she kept me informed and wrote me when he died. Allie died a year ago from Alzheimer's.

This year between high school and college was a lousy year. Two terrible, demoralizing jobs; my hostility toward my mother; and wanting to get on with my life, wanting to get going with college, colored it definitely negative. I suppose I got some good out of it—the bookcase, which I was proud of; my friendship with Allie; and beginning my biographical journal were good growth experiences, especially the concerts with Aunt Bessie.

Mildred — age 18

Barnard College

Barnard College is the undergraduate college for women in Columbia University in New York City. Broadway runs north-south between them. I was on a large scholarship.

Arriving at Barnard was exciting and scary. The dorm floor, however, was very well organized, and the freshmen on that floor had a wonderful second-year student to guide us. Next door to me was another freshman, Mary J., who became my best friend. She's been a friend for many years. The guide, Mary H., also was a long-time friend until she died of breast cancer several years ago.

Before classes started, there was a mixer dance to which Columbia freshmen were invited. I determined to improve my social skills and start a new life, so I went. I met one man who invited me on a date, to drink at a bar. One of his first questions was, did I believe in free love? I was so naïve, I wasn't even sure what he meant. I think I said something like "I don't think so." And at the bar I asked for tomato juice! He was astounded, as was the bartender. That was the end of that.

I joined the Chapel Choir, which required an audition. I passed it! The chapel is on the Columbia campus. Next to Mary J., the choir became my family. It was at the coffee hour there that I learned to drink coffee. After church on Sunday, we went down to Riverside Park and sang. John B., who was a real musician, would lead us. We sang Renaissance and some modern sacred music, and I learned a lot about it and loved it. In my third and fourth years, I had the job of buying refreshments for the Friday pre-rehearsal coffee hour. We rehearsed three afternoons a week plus a pre-church rehearsal on Sundays, and we also sang every noon at a short service. I enjoyed all the gatherings and felt I really belonged. After afternoon rehearsals, the Barnard students of the choir came back to the dorm dining room together, arriving at the last minute of the serving.

I remember my first class, Modern European History, taught by a very good professor with a French accent. But I had never learned in high school to take notes. I learned note-taking fast and bought myself a notebook. (Later my mother told me I shouldn't have bought it because Aunt Bessie was planning to get me one.) I also took third-year Spanish, knowing that my third year in high school was so dismally inadequate. This course was definitely harder. I remember on a test, we were unmonitored because of the Honor Code. Two students talked about their answers. I knew I should tell them I'd report them to the Honor Board, but I couldn't bring myself to do so. Consequently I've carried guilt about it ever since. I read a real book in Spanish, not a text, and understood most of it, and then passed the "exit exam," a foreign language being a college requirement. But I could never converse in Spanish.

I think it was at Thanksgiving break that Mom again offered, or rather requested, to massage my feet. For the previous years when she did that, she had wanted it to take place at her and Dad's bed, and Dad often fell asleep. What really bothered me was the apparent, to me, sexual implications of being in their bed, and it was why I did so much sleeping away from home. This time, instead of responding docilely, I gave her a sharp rebuke, and she never asked again. I wish I hadn't been so sharp, but the result was what I wanted.

I met a senior student, Isabel (Izzie) S., and she became very quickly a special friend. She was more idealistic than others, and I had a real crush. At first she was very outgoing, but gradually became more withdrawn. I worried about her increasingly. Over the Christmas holiday, she stayed with another friend and became seriously depressed. As I learned upon return to school, she had been hospitalized in a psychiatric unit. I was devastated and worried, and I couldn't eat. I tried to maintain contact with letters, and in the spring she did return, with a much reduced class schedule. She was able to graduate with her class.

I asked my parents if she could spend the summer with us, since her mother lived far away and she had a new job in New York. They agreed, and she really became part of our family, especially with my dad. They kept up a friendship until my dad died; she took part in his funeral. That summer she slept in my sister's bedroom; Frances was working in the Poconos at the Antlers Inn.

The job I had was in New York City, and so I commuted again. I had to type the same letter to send to hundreds of chemists. There were no copiers then. It was boring but easy. The office was high up in an office building near the Public Library, Grand Central, and a Movietone place. I often spent my lunch hour at Movietone, keeping up with the news and also in the large garden (Bryant Park) behind the Library.

At the end of the summer, I drove with my parents to Louisiana to visit Uncle Fletcher (Mom's brother) and his family. Izzie had left for an apartment in New York near her job. Frances was working at the Antlers Inn in the Poconos. My memory is that she did not come with us but Frances remembers that she did. There was another trip there before or later, which maybe explains the discrepancy. We camped out on the trip, sleeping in the truck and making campfires. One night we heard a whippoorwill calling. The visit was a good one. I talked with the grandson, Wally, who was a teen, about race relations. His parents and grandparents were pretty conservative, but Wally had thought a lot about it and I was encouraged by his more tolerant attitude.

One of our sight-seeing trips while visiting was south to and into the Mississippi Delta. My main memory from that was my need for a bathroom, which no one else in the car needed (I think I was the only female). The only resource was a run-down outhouse way behind a run-down gas station. I had to get there through mud and high grass. The mosquitoes were so thick I could have grabbed handfuls, and as a captive in the outhouse my back was totally vulnerable. Again, I was stung all over my back. I had always reacted to even single mosquito bites with a lot of inflammation, as if I was allergic to them— they always got inflamed and swollen. Again when we finally got home, I was put to bed on my stomach with medicine and wet towels on my back.

I, an inexperienced driver, drove the car home. In passing a truck too closely, I ripped off our door handle. Dad had warned me to no avail. But he was not judgmental.

When we returned to Chatham, a letter was waiting for me from a young man in the choir. He was somewhat eccentric. The letter was asking me to give him more time, and he gave odd reasons (that each course I had taken represented an attribute of my character) that were strange. In psychiatric terms, they were "ideas of reference." On return to school, I told him his feelings were more strong than mine. He accepted this, but I know he was quite disappointed. I knew there had to be something wrong with a man who was attracted to me.

At the beginning of my sophomore year, I was still worried about Izzie and became depressed. I was rooming with Mary J., and I felt she was distancing from me. I went to the school doctor and got one sleeping pill. Later I went back to her, and I was so scared after she closed her office door, I ran out of her office. The depression gradually lifted. I was taking music appreciation, which I loved. It helped me regain my composure.

That year I still had phys. ed. requirements and played badminton a lot. I got to be very skillful at it. As in field hockey, it required more quick movements than running. This time my feet hung in there.

One time Mary J., who had visited at my home for a few days, and I were returning to college on a rainy Sunday evening. We had to walk from the ferry to the subway, going through a deserted warehouse area of the Bowery. We saw several men on the ground beside a building. One was lying in a puddle; they were all dead drunk. I put down my suitcase and tried to sit him up out of the puddle. He was a deadweight, but he did say enough to me to indicate he appreciated my concern. I couldn't get him fully out of the puddle, but did the best I could. Mary hung back, telling me not to do this. I think she was afraid of them.

At the end of the year, with exams, I became depressed again. I had wanted to take my third year off, as money was very tight, and work. My mother dissuaded me. Her letter saying this would hurt my friends caused me to become depersonalized for several days. I think that was one cause for the depression. This was the time I went to Aunt Bessie's apartment. I had tried unsuccessfully to get a summer job, and my mother thought I shouldn't work.

Finally, late in the summer I had an opportunity to be Ruth Webb's necessary companion for two weeks. Ruth was the daughter of the Antlers owners, Mr. and Mrs. Webb, who had been college friends of Aunt Bessie. She was the girl I'd learned about from Aunt Bessie's friend's visit when I was in high school. Ruth was severely handicapped with cerebral palsy and needed almost constant help. That talented, gutsy, and courageous woman, in spite of her severe handicap, went on to get her Ph.D. and had an illustrious career as a researcher in special education. I went to her eightieth birthday party recently, given by Dave (her brother and Fran's husband) at Andra's home (Frances' oldest daughter). It was a grand party, with great tributes to Ruth. Of those two weeks we were together, the first week we spent at New York University where she was taking a course, and the second week at the Antlers.

Frances was at the Inn also for the summer, as a waitress. She was getting acquainted with Dave, Ruth's brother, whom she much later married. A memorable incident occurred while we were there. Frances got bitten by a bee and quickly became very sick, with her throat closing up so she couldn't breathe. I was called, and Mr. Webb drove us several miles to the home (it was dinnertime) of the nearest doctor. By the time we got there Fran was really collapsing. The doctor took us promptly and gave her an adrenaline shot. She got nauseated, but resting on the doctor's couch, she gradually recovered and we went back to the Inn. The doctor did not charge us. My depression lifted during that week, as I was being useful to both Fran and Ruth.

My third year was a good year by and large. I financed it with loans from the college. In the fall, I was elected by my floormates to monitor bed-making. They thought I wouldn't do a thing. I fooled them and gave lots of warnings! I chose physics as my major. There was only one other physics major, Gladys Lerner. Consequently we spent much time together. We weren't really close, and the only time I ever saw her again was at our fiftieth anniversary.

I developed a crush on a female classmate in the choir, who was a writer and quite troubled emotionally. We became quite close, and I worried about her too.

Gypsy

There was a young man in the choir, Ken, on whom I also had a crush. He became aware of my crush and out of kindness took me out for a date. We had spaghetti dinner at his apartment. When we returned to my dorm, he kissed me! I was so thrilled my adrenaline was pumping and I stayed up all night. I was afraid I'd wake Mary and so spent the night sitting on steps in the stairwell. Later I had two wisdom teeth pulled and spent a day or two in the infirmary. But Ken did not visit me, as I had hoped he would.

At the end of that year, I got a job as mother's helper with a family who were counseling and administrative staff at Teachers' College (part of Columbia). They had two adopted children, Jack, seven, and Peggy, five or six. They took me to their summer cabin in an exclusive place in the Adirondacks between the Hudson and Connecticut. At first it seemed like an ideal placement, and I was very happy. Jack had severe asthma and usually woke and cried out in the night. My room was next to his and I was glad to go give him his inhaler and reassure him. One night, however, his mother beat me to it. I heard her yell at and scold him, that he could get his inhaler by himself. He never called for me again. I observed his mother rationing her love for him at certain brief times, and her obvious pride in her daughter, whose beauty she admired. Peggy was a delightful little girl, but I was sad to see Jack become more and more fearful of things. Once I was late in bringing the kids back for dinner, and the mother was furious at me; I certainly deserved it.

In the lodge, a building open to all, down near the lake, was a piano. The mother knew I had taken piano lessons and suggested I teach Jack and Peggy. I thought I could, because I well remembered my first lessons with Mrs. Smith. We made a couple of attempts, but the children were not really interested. It got no farther.

Toward the end of summer, my parents came for a day and I was given a day off, the only one I got all summer. We got a rowboat and went out on the lake. I believe that was the occasion when Mom told me that Gypsy had died, a natural death. Gypsy had been essentially immobilized for some time with aging, lying on her rug by the radiator in the kitchen. Whenever I came home, she couldn't move her body, but would bang her tail on the floor to greet me. My mother loved her, and Gypsy's death was a deep loss for her.

The exclusive village I was staying in housed many rich folk. The young people saw me as a maid and ignored me completely. By summer's end I was very glad to come home.

My fourth college year was exciting. My major was in physics, but about Thanksgiving time, talking with a group of friends—pre-med majors—I said, "Sometimes I wish I was pre-med."

Charlotte said, "You really could with the science background you have. Why don't you?" and I began thinking about it. I had no idea what I would do after graduation with a physics major (maybe do something in acoustics?)

and I was ripe for such an idea. I went to bed, thought a lot, and stayed awake most of the night from the adrenaline, and by morning had made up my mind. My reasons for choosing medicine were my history of orthopedic problems and my admiration of Dr. Barnett; my need to know the details and the truth; my awareness that the appendectomy had been foisted on me for no good reason, and also the T&As on Billie and Fran; my high school interest in chemotherapy; and my finding that I had an interest in listening and talking to troubled people. Mostly, I wanted to serve.

The next day I went about changing my courses to get in one more pre-med one. I had started to take qualitative analysis at Columbia and got straight A's. I switched to quantitative, which was more required than qual. Back across Broadway at Barnard, I had trouble from the beginning. I think that was one of the B's. By the second semester, I realized I wouldn't be able to do two required courses (zoology and embryology) and also owed Barnard some loan money and had none for medical school. I began thinking about ways to manage this, but never gave up on med school.

I came across a bulletin board notice from Mount Holyoke College, advertising for students to get their Master's degrees in two years while being paid as assistant instructors. In my case, it would be in the physics department. I applied and asked to be able to also take those two pre-med courses in the zoology department. I was accepted after an interview there.

In my second senior semester at Barnard, I was chosen to head up preparations for an intercollegiate science fair. Several students were preparing good projects to exhibit, and I enjoyed supervising them. I scheduled ten-minute meetings with them and others between my classes, so I was constantly running. I got the glass-blower at Columbia, whom I knew from previous contacts, to agree to do a demonstration for an audience on the last day. I made a big mistake in that I was so tired I failed to show for his demonstration.

Afterward my advisor told me what I had done wrong. I was quite chagrined. The man had come on stage late, after waiting for me to introduce him, and done a half-hearted demonstration. Mortified, I went to apologize to him.

There was one boy from Union College at the science fair who seemed to take a liking to me. I asked someone who knew him if he was "sincere." She said no, which was all the excuse I needed to avoid further contact with him. My social skills still needed working on.

Also toward the end of that year I organized a group of students who wanted to visit a mental hospital. At that time the only mental hospital I had any knowledge of was Greystone in New Jersey, out beyond Morristown. Part of my purpose was to include Ken, who was a psychology major. (He later became a psychoanalyst.) I had on a pink skirt. One of the men with us said it looked like that was my slip. I was embarrassed for the rest of the trip.

We went by train out to Morris Plains, I think. My friend Ruth found out about our plan and wanted to come too. She met us at the hospital. I don't remember how she got there. We announced ourselves, and the director met with us. As soon as he saw Ruth's wheelchair he said to me that she couldn't come in. I think I did some mild questioning, but he was adamant. Ruth was quite upset. If I said that "all of us wouldn't," then it would be negative for all the others too. I wasn't strong enough to really remonstrate, so we left Ruth there. I felt very unhappy about that.

We were taken through two or three wards. In one there was a platform at one end of the dayroom, and a woman was singing operatic arias but ignored us. Other women were sitting on the floor, backs against the wall, sitting in many positions. Some sat with their legs akimbo, showing us they had no underpants on. It was quite demoralizing. We met Ruth again when we left, but I don't remember how we all got back. Ruth has had a very illustrious career after getting her Ph.D. in special education, as a staff member and researcher at a Developmental Center in Iowa. She has now retired and has written her autobiography too and a couple of more recent books.

We didn't have grade-point averages then, but I graduated after getting one C and a couple of B's for the four years, the rest being A's. The C was in music theory, from third year. I had to take the GRE (Graduate Record Exam) in lieu of a written physics exam. I believe I aced it but never got a score. I also had to take an oral exam. I was questioned by my two physics professors. It was miserable. I sat on a high stool, and I remember the plaid skirt I had on. I was scared to death. They asked almost all history of physics questions. I don't think I was able to answer a single one. The professors were kind. I think they did not include that in their final grade. I was very proud of my A.B. (*Ars Batcheloris*—Latin) degree. My parents, Frances, Auntie Nan, and Aunt Muriel attended the ceremonies.

Sally L. the troubled writer and opera-lover, took offense to a poor comment of mine. She was writing a book about the Vikings, and I said the chapters were non-sequential. She heard it as 'inconsequential' and immediately dropped me. I couldn't persuade her otherwise. I called her once after graduation at her job, and she really had no interest in seeing me. That was the end of that.

That summer I got another mother's helper job with a Manhattan French family at their summer house in the Hamptons (another exclusive area) on Long Island. There was a new baby, two or three weeks old at the time of my interview, and a three-year-old girl, Christie, who was just beginning to learn to speak French. Since I didn't, she pretty much stopped speaking.

The mother's mother had recently had a big back operation, was bedridden, would come to the Long Island place, and was said to be a tyrant. I was to feed the baby, take care of the little girl, and do errands. It again started out well, but after the grandmother came, the mother spent most time with her and I really had the care of the children. When the grandmother arrived and had to be gotten into a wheelchair and then into her bedroom, the girl's father was very busy with the proceedings and asked me to take the little girl away without his speaking to her first. Christie cried frantically for him until finally he returned from the grandmother's room. Then he finally came back and talked with Christie for a long time. I felt very empathetic with Christie during all this, and it was all I could do to keep her away.

The little girl was a darling, and we became fast friends. I took her when I drove to do errands. I fed the baby, who was kept in his carriage otherwise. He was a passive baby, and when the mother took him to the pediatrician, she was told he was not getting enough stimulation. She was frightened and then kept him with her and the grandmother.

During that summer, a friend of the mother (a real princess, I was told) came to stay for a while. I fantasized getting close to her and then having her finance my medical education! My fantasies came to naught. Late one afternoon she came into the kitchen where I was, scooped up all the spaghetti on the stove—which I had planned to eat for my supper—and ate it cold. Afterwards, the mother found me crying in the kitchen. I told her why, and she whipped up some eggs for my supper. She was very thoughtful, and I liked her.

One day Christie went with me to get groceries. On our way back to the car, with my arms full of bags, I couldn't hang onto her too, and she suddenly ran out into the street between parked cars. Frantically I chased her. Fortunately the car coming was able to stop. Somehow I finally got her and the groceries into our car. Another time, I was driving along a wooded road with her beside me, and she opened her door and began to lean out. I grabbed her by the clothes and brought the car to a stop. I pulled her back in, closed the door, and scolded her gently. Being truthful, I told her mother about both incidents. It was toward the end of the summer, and she didn't send me on any more errands. Whenever I hear someone oppose seat belts and car seats for children, I think of that close call.

One Episcopal church there held summer services with a choir, which I joined. Although I enjoyed the singing, I was looked down upon as a maid, getting minimal attention from the members. It was quite familiar.

Again, not having my own car to drive, my parents came in the delivery truck to take me back home. It was a sad goodbye, because I knew the little girl didn't understand I was leaving and would miss me terribly. I have often wondered how those children and the two from the year before ever made out. I never heard again from either family.

I kept up with a few other choir friends after college: Sally S., Kris (and later her husband Steve), Mac (and her husband John, the same one who led us singing in the park), and Barbara (and her husband John). When we started having choir reunions in the 1970s, I remade acquaintance with all these and many others too, especially Fran A. From outside the choir, I continued friendships with the two Marys.

Those were four years of much growth and learning, and the memories are vivid and lasting. I developed a number of female friendships, but I still had a long ways to go socially.

Depression

Depression has been a frequent companion throughout my life. I think the first one occurred when I was in the hospital at age four, and the second one during my third year at Camp Morris. Because I was quiet and said little, no one picked it up, not that anyone would have in those years. I have almost always been able to conceal depression, because I'm generally quiet and don't show my feelings. I can cry completely silently, at least until I have to blow my nose. I can put on my professional persona when seeing patients.

I remember choosing navy blue fabric for a craft project at the camp. I thought it was blue and was disappointed to see it when it came. I said it wasn't what I wanted and the counselor scolded me. When we went home after the third week, I felt no joy at seeing my parents. I felt depersonalized (like a robot) for a few days. Entering junior high restored me.

The next time was at Camp Mogisca, the Girl Scout camp, the next summer. Aunt Bessie helped me deal with that by her surprising visit midterm. Summers tended to be problematic; in spite of my shyness, I really enjoyed school. Eleanor and Gloria helped a lot the semester I was casted at home. The whole year after graduation and before college was between very bad and not-so-bad. Allie helped me through that.

In college, I developed an early crush on an upper classwoman, Izzie, who became mentally ill, reaching a crisis with hospitalization during Christmas vacation. When I returned to school after Christmas, and learned what happened I was really distraught. I couldn't eat. As I began to hear from her and learned she was better and coming back to school, I began to feel better. The following summer I invited her to spend the summer with my family, who took her in readily. Although I worried about her, I was okay until I returned for my sophomore year. I felt depressed from the start and went to see the school doctor. After I sat down and told her my friends didn't like me, she got up and closed the door. I panicked and ran from the room. When I get very depressed I get paranoid, which happens in some cases of severe depression. That depression lasted a few weeks. Once, I went into Low Library, which had a huge rotunda and stairs going up against the walls. On the stairs, I heard a whisper from the opposite wall, saying, "Won't you, Millie, come and follow me?" I knew it was an illusion, not true, but it was food for thought.

At the end of that year was when I got quite depressed and went to Aunt Bessie's apartment, and she came back to school with me the next day. She was a tremendous help, but the depression continued into the summer. I had failed to find a summer job, and my parents wanted me to stay home. I worried over finances and college expenses. My father came to my room one time while I was obsessing about it to assure me that we could handle the expenses. It helped but I knew it wasn't true. Later I thought about loans.

In August I had an opportunity to spend two weeks with Ruth, a friend who was disabled with cerebral palsy and needed constant companionship and help. Her parents paid me.

The first week she and I were at a class in social questions at New York University for which she got college credit. I grew very fond of Ruth, but it was not a crush. She was five years older than I. The second week we spent at her parents' summer inn. Spending those weeks helping Ruth helped me a lot. Returning to college for my third year, I did much better. (See also "Barnard College.")

I got through the next two years okay, with some blues at times. The next real depression I had was when I was at Mount Holyoke College for two years. I started off all right but quickly became very depressed. One Saturday afternoon I slept for four hours. I went to the school doctor, and after some tests, she diagnosed hypothyroidism. The BMR (Basal Metabolism Rate was the primary test then) was minus 31, very low. She prescribed thyroid, which I took until the prescription ran out. The doctor had not given me follow-up instructions. Feeling it had not helped I did not return to her or continue the meds. I gradually got better. Depression never caused me to miss school or not complete my work, but it felt as if I were in a deep dark well, with no escape. The physical feeling of depression is of a continuously crushed chest, a foggy brain, and utter exhaustion.

The second year there was better, as I was working on getting into med school. However the group of grad students I lived with really ostracized me and laughed at my poor social skills. I cried at times but got through.

The first year in med school I had the worst and longest-lasting depression that I had ever had. I ate poorly, thinking I was being frugal, and got vitamin deficiencies. A friend, Nancy R., who was a third year student, helped me a great deal (see also the chapter on "Medical School"). Finally she talked to me about seeing a psychiatrist. I had no trouble agreeing to it, and she helped make arrangements. Early in the second semester I started seeing Dr. Charles Richards, of whom I became very fond. He helped me a lot and gave me amphetamines for a few weeks, which only made me feel jittery, but the depression stayed.

At the end of that year, Dr. Richards was on vacation, and I was supposed to start a summer research job in physiology. On a weekend with almost no one around in the dorm, I really felt I might commit suicide by jumping out my open window. I found a graduating senior and got her to come and close my window. She took over and got me hospitalized at Payne Whitney, the psychiatric unit of New York Hospital. For the first day I cried a lot. I couldn't see Dr. Richards because he was not on staff, and I felt very paranoid. I ostensibly cooperated with my assigned resident, but was reticent with him about important issues.

At the beginning of August, with much persuasion on my part, they let me visit my sister in Philadelphia, who was having her first baby. I was very anxious while there, but she said I helped her, and I returned to the hospital with renewed self-esteem. Then they got Dr. Richards on staff so I could see him. Then I really got better, and though still officially in the hospital as classes started, attended them all and soon went back to my dorm room. I continued to see Dr. Richards for the next three years, but had no significant depression. My medical school classmates knew what happened, but were always respectful and friendly to me. I deeply appreciate their compassion. One even shook my hand as we returned that fall. Our particular class was excellent.

After med school, where I graduated in the third quarter (not the fourth!) of seventy-six students, I moved to Rochester for my internship. For the first six months I was on psychiatry. I had no depression to speak of for several months and got married in March. At that time I was on pediatrics, where I did not do well at all. I goofed on some important cases, couldn't tolerate the lack of sleep, and missed some classes because of lack of sleep. I got quite depressed. My husband did not know what to do with me. He tried to be empathetic with me about this, but being empathic was not his forte. I felt I had to quit the internship after one year, which was supposed to be for two years. After quitting, I got pregnant and continued to be very depressed almost throughout the pregnancy, feeling very guilty for deserting my intern cohort in the middle of the two years. I gained forty pounds eating ham and couldn't make myself do housework until my husband reprimanded me. I was not seeing any therapist. Toward the end of the pregnancy I began to feel better, and when the baby came, enjoyed him except for "first baby anxieties."

Soon there were real anxieties about the baby. He turned out to be not normal, and at three months, we institutionalized him. I soon got pregnant again and remained depressed. I got a part-time job at the University of Rochester Psychiatry Department's Therapeutic Nursery, examining newly admitted children. This was a very rewarding experience but the depression did not lift. I began taking too much time from the Director, who was a wonderful kindly woman.

Again I felt better by the time of the second baby. I worried about her because of the first baby's problems, but was not seriously depressed. I moved with my husband and baby to a house in Greece (a suburb of Rochester). We had a third baby and I did okay for a while. I became very active in our church, which was partly denial of difficulties at home. Finally my husband scolded me for not doing enough mothering duties. So I cut back and cried a lot. Depression gradually deepened, and finally in 1963 when the youngest baby was two years old, I started therapy, against my husband's wishes, with Dr. Myrtle Pleune.

She was very helpful, and in 1965 I was able to start a part-time job at the local state hospital, again against my husband's wishes, though I wanted to earn enough to pay for my therapy. I continued therapy until mid-1968, when I felt well enough to go it alone.

I continued my job and started a private practice in 1969 in Rochester, which was very exciting. I then did well until 1979, when I began to make several changes in my life. I separated from my husband, quit the State Hospital job and took another in a new Community Mental Health Center, and moved to an apartment. At that time I did get depressed again, mostly over the separation, leaned on my director at the mental health center, and finally started therapy again with Dr. Joyce DuBrin, a psychologist. She again was very helpful. Soon I started in group therapy with her and her husband, Bob Pierce, Ph.D. I participated actively in the therapy, and it became a very important part of my life. In the mid-80s, I realized that Joyce's presence kept me from being depressed, when she went on two vacations with a week in between. The one week she was back I felt better. I then started an anti-depressant. It definitely helped after a few weeks. It's surprising in retrospect that I'd never considered this before. At RPC depressed patients were worse than I, mute and unresponsive, but even later it took me a long time to realize my depression was bad enough to warrant antidepressants.

I continued with Joyce and doing better until 1990, when I made a decision to change the medical group I was working with. Dr. DuBrin (Joyce) forced me to terminate therapy, which was very upsetting, telling me the session after my announcement. That was a weird session. I was frantic. I depersonalized right through it, feeling I was in the opposite corner looking at me and Joyce. I became a basket case. (See "Continuing Changes".)

While I was in the process of termination, I started therapy with Dr. Ray Babineau, a psychiatrist. It took two years to get over Joyce's rejection, but since then, continuing with Ray and taking the anti-depressants, I have not had any significant depression, with one exception after 9/11, which affected me strongly. On my next visit to Rochester, Ray talked to me about it, and I started a second anti-depressant. Since then, I have done well.

In retrospect, I wonder if the depressions had anything to do with my never feeling much grief after a family death. The time when I went to Rochester after my mother died may be indicative of that. I felt no grief at the time of her death, but after coming to Rochester I had trouble dealing with the young mother patient admitted to our floor and was depressed. Also, I grieved after Joyce's rejection and Lou's death when I was taking anti-depressants, and I had no other depressions. On the other hand, my father's death was after I was taking anti-depressants and my grief was minimal, so the theory doesn't completely hold. This is only a theory. Since taking them and since the two years of grief about Joyce, I haven't cried at all, even when I had hard times. However, I tear up and sob a little when I learn about certain types of *positive* human interest stories—like heroes, children, animals, patriotic acts, or certain music, like the songs in *Sound of Music* or *Madame Butterfly*.

The Master's Program at Mount Holyoke

From B+ to C-

There were seven or eight grad students in the first year of the program, and we were housed together in the Faculty House. I was the only one in physics; the others were all chemistry and zoology. Janet, one of the zo assistants, had the room next to mine, a suite with bathroom between. I did become friends with her, but not the others. We got small stipends from the college, enough for me to pay off my loans. In the Physics Department, I did pretty well. I supervised the one lab for first-year physics students. I was supposed to attend their lectures too, but they were at 8 A.M. I got to one or two. I had never had to deal with eight o'clocks at Barnard and couldn't deal with it at Mount Holyoke. I didn't really need the lectures to manage the lab, and I was never called on it by Mildred Allen, the Chair.

I enjoyed helping the students in the labs. One student named Nancy asked me many many questions. I finally pointed out to her that she was capable of getting them right, and did, on her own every time, to encourage her to be more independent. She took me seriously and thereafter did very well. I also enjoyed being called "Professor Moore."

I had to pass an oral test in German, required mainly to be able to read scientific articles. I had never taken German, but brought a text with me. I studied it on my own, and toward the end of the year Miss Allen asked me to translate an article. I aced it, but never spoke it!

As planned, I took zoology the first year and embryology the second year. I did very well and enjoyed both. Once I acted as a substitute residence counselor for one night at an upperclass dormitory. It was interesting to listen to the girls. They took good care of me!

In physics, I took quantum mechanics and one or two other courses from Professor Ed Clancy. I had a book of Niels Bohr lectures, compiled by his students. They had made many, many mistakes in their math (I wondered if they really understood it). I went through the book and corrected every mistake. Professor Clancy was very impressed.

In the Department was a second year master's student, Ann. We became pretty good friends, and I've kept up with her. One time, when I finally had a boyfriend (Martin) in med school, I got her to drive him and me to Tanglewood for a concert that I particularly wanted to hear, the Berlioz Requiem. Why she drove us, I don't know. It was obviously a ruse on my part.

Meanwhile, in the Faculty Residence at Mount Holyoke, I quickly was thought of by the other grads as quite eccentric. Dinners were especially traumatic for me. Most of the time I said nothing, but once in a while initiated a topic which never got going. One time I told what I thought was a joke, expecting laughter. There was none, and my eyes filled with tears with the realization that they were trying to hold back laughter. I left my dinner and ran up to my room, and on the way I heard them laughing uproariously at me.

The first fall didn't start well. I decided to try to go to a dance at Amherst College. Janet promised to find me a date. That took a long time, and I changed my mind about going and tried to stop it, but Janet misunderstood me and she and others tried even harder. Finally they found someone, who was a real loser and actually stank. At the dance I suffered immensely. It was horrible. Depression was deepening (see that chapter).

Meanwhile, I had become friends with a botany professor who lived down the hall from me. She was a brittle diabetic and easily depressed. We became a mutually supportive pair, and I had quite a crush on her. It was she I ran to from that dinner. She was prone to insulin seizures. One night Janet woke me because she could hear Eva having a seizure on the other side of the wall. I went to her room and gave her orange juice and stayed with her a while. She was in close contact with her doctor, but had many seizures anyway. I showed her my outline of a lecture I'd heard, written after it was over. She was quite impressed with my ability to get it all down. That speaker was very well organized!

One of the other grad students, Peggy, I thought was becoming more and more aloof from the group. I took it on myself to find her alone in her room and discussed it with her. It sounds strange, given my social role with the group, but she took me seriously. It was a good conversation, she said, helpful to her. Peggy later drove me to the train station in Holyoke. She said that as thanks I might help someone else out. The twenty dollars I had for my Christmas break train ticket home—all I had—was stolen from a coat rack. I must have then borrowed someone's money. Later the wallet was returned, dirty and sticky, with no cash.

I had to write a thesis, and after much debate decided to build a scintillation counter, made with a radioactive crystal and electronics to sense, amplify, and record the decay impulses. The summer after the first year I spent in New York living with Izzie and another roommate. I worked at

Women's Hospital as an operating room orderly and had very early hours. I spent the afternoons in the Columbia physics library, researching everything I could about building the counter. I had a terrible time staying awake because of the early hours, but I believe I got all the notes I needed. I started actually building the counter my second year.

The second year the grads were housed in an empty house a ways away. I had the only room on the third floor. The others did not like some of my habits, like my not cleaning the tub after I bathed. It was called to my attention by Janet, who seemed to be an intermediary, and then I did better. I became more and more isolated, except from Janet. I also became friends with a gym instructor who also wanted to go to med school and was quite troubled. One day she had an hysterical paralysis and created quite a commotion. I listened a lot to her painful revelations. I never heard from her after that year.

I built the scintillation counter. There were a lot of things about it that needed correction, but finally at the end of the year, it was working and I calibrated it. I stayed after graduation trying to improve it. Finally I decided I'd had enough, and left. I learned later from Professor Clancy that it still wasn't completely all right. However the relief I felt on leaving it was a major revelation to me. I had always wanted to finish anything I started, even when it dragged on and on. This was a new experience. Only once before, with my National Geographic project, had I not finished. It later happened a few more times.

That second semester, I made applications to four med schools—Cornell, University of Rochester, University of Syracuse, and I forget the fourth (possibly P&S, of Columbia). I had to write an essay about myself. In it I mentioned my ability and interest in listening to troubled people and wish to serve. In the spring I traveled to each school for interviews and apparently did okay, but was not accepted by the last two (actually interviewed first) because of lack of financing. At the University of Rochester, I was interviewed by Dean Whipple himself, who told me that they would accept me when I got the money. I had managed to pay off all my loans, but still had no other resources. I contacted a number of foundations and funds without luck.

The last interview I went to was Cornell. I was interviewed by two professors at the hospital, then sent to see Dr. Connie Guion in her private office. She had already talked to the other two interviewers and after a brief interview offered me a full four-year scholarship, which would pay all my expenses! That was, of course, a tremendous load off my back.

Back at Mount Holyoke, when the other grad students learned of my success, they were flabbergasted, Janet said. They thought no way could I be accepted, much less get such a scholarship. Again, my parents and the two aunts attended my graduation, when I got my Master of Arts degree in physics. I stayed those few extra days, then went home by train.

My Spiritual Autobiography

Most of this chapter was originally written as part of a short course at my church in my sixties.

I grew up in St. Paul's Episcopal Church in Chatham, which my grandfather co-founded. Frances and I attended regularly. I believed in the personal God I learned about and prayed to. When I was five or six, I asked my mother if she believed in God. Her answer reflected my beginning sense of doubt, that she believed in a Presence one calls God, but not a person. So then, "Why pray?"

"Because it makes you think," she answered.

The church was small as churches go. Uncle George (Aunt Gladys' husband) was Superintendent of the Sunday School. I remember his pride the first time attendance hit 100!

The minister was Dr. Guy Emery Shipler. He did not call himself a priest. He didn't talk much about God or the Bible, as I recall, except with the prayers and ritual responses as part of every service. But he did talk about service, social and political issues, and countering evil things and people. He was very liberal, and the church was "low Episcopalian." His very strong opinions caused dissension in the congregation. He preached equality among the races and many in our congregation weren't ready for that.

When I finished Sunday School at eighth grade, Aunt Sallie persuaded me to join the adult choir, of which she was a major part, and I attended regularly. I was formally confirmed in the Episcopal Church by the Bishop. At the time I was sincere about that. When I was in high school, Dr. Shipler was vehemently criticized and ridiculed by many parishioners, including some in the choir who made comments at every opportunity, whispering and giggling, with derisive smiles during his sermons. He had a profound influence on me and shaped my support of social justice, and this injustice pained me greatly.

He was finally driven from the church. I went off to college so I had to face the new priest only three or four times. He was very religious and ended his services with "Thanks be to God who giveth us the victory," meaning the end of the war as well as the traditional meaning. My reaction was that God isn't on one side or the other, and the priest really revolted me.

At college I joined the Chapel Choir, High Episcopalian, which quickly became my most active extracurricular activity. Because of the earlier molestation episode (see "The Pubertal Years"), and Dr. Shipler's experience, I was down on priests. I ignored all sermons and never made acquaintance with the priest. But I came to revere sacred music and was intensely involved in choir activities. Music came to symbolize my inherent spiritual feelings, but I had no interest in the prayers, rituals, creed, etc. In graduate school I sometimes went into the Mount Holyoke chapel to meditate but attended no services.

The summer after I finished grad school, because service had become the primary purpose of my spiritual life, I enrolled in the AFSC (American Friends Service Committee) Summer Project. I worked at a state hospital in Connecticut as a lowly attendant, but was one of a group of like-minded young adults working in different buildings. Every day after work we met and sat silently in a circle for meditation. There was some conversation about religious values, and we learned about the Friends' beliefs and customs, thus enriching my ideas about service and spirituality. I had no interest in any formal church, but the Quaker way intrigued me greatly. We once visited a Quaker couple who lived nearby.

In medical school I was too busy for any religious activities, but I was preparing myself for a profession of service. In Rochester for my internship, I became engaged and my fiancé learned of the First Unitarian Church. He heard primarily about the lack of a creed and the support of science. As I looked into it I realized that it really demonstrated an emphasis on service and love, with the "no creed and the respect for modern science" being more peripheral. We were married in the Unitarian Church by Dr. David Rhys Williams, a fact that I am proud of. Dr. Williams had almost identical attitudes as Dr. Shipler had.

The Seven Principles of Unitarian-Universalism are:

1. The inherent worth and dignity of every person;
2. Justice, equity, and compassion in human relations;
3. Acceptance of one another and encouragement to spiritual growth in our congregations;
4. A free and responsible search for truth and meaning;
5. The right of conscience and the use of the democratic process within our congregations and in society at large;
6. The goal of world community with peace, liberty, and justice for all;
7. Respect for the interdependent web of all existence, of which we are a part.

When I decided to go into psychiatry, it fulfilled my need to provide service. Also, I think there's a spiritual component to work of this kind, and it fits several of the Unitarian Principles. A major theme of my journey, spiritual and otherwise, had been the search for truth, which is what psychotherapy is all about. For fifteen years I worked at Rochester Psychiatric Center. I began in various ways to advocate for the mentally ill. There I met the Protestant chaplain and we developed a friendship as I began to readjust my attitudes toward ministers. Together we started a support group for patients' families, the primary topic being transition from in-patient to outpatient status. At that time I was not attending church but my children were attending the First Unitarian Church School, because I transported them.

In 1990 I suffered a terrible loss of faith and confidence in someone I had greatly loved and admired (Joyce—see chapter on "Continuing Changes"). This event set off a great grief, and I felt devastated. It sent me back to the church, where I realized how important its community is, both specifically and as a general concept. I rejoined the choir and found there a wonderful community and a very good choir and Director. It was said to be the best choir in Rochester.

In 1996, Lou, my best friend and soulmate, died. At the next choir rehearsal, Ed Schell embraced me, and the members were very supportive. About that time, I took a one-session course about one's spiritual autobiography. Our church encourages people to think those things out for ourselves, with the major emphasis on love, service, and justice. Those events in my life started me thinking more closely about the meanings of my spirituality, and ready to work out the details.

So I then took a course on "Building Your Own Theology," taught by our minister, Dr. Richard Gilbert, which was very enlightening. I believe there's some spirit that connects all living creatures. It's an interconnecting web. That enters my thoughts in connection with our earth's environmental problems, which I think are the most significant problems our planet is facing. This interconnecting presence could be responsible for the occasional psychic phenomena, even dream messages, that do occur. It might be a kind of pseudo/electromagnetic field, in which impulses can be transmitted over long distances. Maybe some day the neuroscientists will figure it out or even find it involved in "string theory" or the "theory of everything" being worked on now by mathematicians. It could also account for some "mystical" experiences, although I think most of those are basically psychological. This might be like an altered state of consciousness.

Spurred by writing my autobiography, I've thought about the misdeeds that I repent the most: my lack of communication with my mother and aunts at the times of their deaths, and not responding to someone's sorrow and grief. I'm still thinking.

CORNELL UNIVERSITY MEDICAL COLLEGE
(now Weill Cornell Medical College)

Cornell Medical College is in New York City, combined with New York Hospital, the teaching hospital. Also the Hospital for Special Surgery was built nearby while I was there.

The first year started off quite well. Most of my classmates were men of course, and I was determined to be natural with them. In anatomy lab, we were paired two persons to a cadaver. My partner was one of the five women, but at the next table was a young man from Florida named Aubrey. I made friends with him, and he invited me to take a drive with him. He had an errand to do at P&S (the Columbia University medical school). I went with him in his beat-up Beetle. We had a good conversation, and we did a few other things together, like go in a group to a seafood restaurant a few blocks from the school. Soon, however, our studies became too onerous to allow outings. In addition, I began to get depressed.

We five women did several of our classes together, without the men, such as physical examination. We became good friends. I felt no indifference, much less any hostility. One—Anne—became close to me. She was going through a difficult time, as her husband was showing the first signs (but soon progressing rapidly) of multiple sclerosis. We have remained friends until now.

One of our courses was Comprehensive Care, for which each student was assigned a family who attended the clinics. We were also to make home visits. My family was Greek and included parents and two young children. I got to know the mother quite well, less so the father. The mother wanted children, the father did not. The mother confided that in order to get pregnant, she had put pinholes in his condoms!

I began to feel I had to be frugal because of the scholarship, and I dieted excessively, to the point of developing vitamin deficiencies. Also I took to taking cold showers in the morning, but soon gave that up. Several events in my family occurred that didn't help, although they did not cause the depression. Both my mother and Aunt Bessie had their first cancer surgeries. I called Aunt Bessie's surgeon, who told me he did a standard radical mastectomy. I was concerned because I had read that mediastinal (in the chest) metastases are frequent, and the surgeon was ignoring it. Both my sister and friend Izzie got married. I was Maid of Honor for each. Frances's reception was held at our house, with so many (hundreds?) present no one could hardly move. I was glad when all these events were over.

I found another friend, Nancy, whose dorm room was next door to mine, who was an upperclassman. I began to spend an inordinate time in the evenings leaning on her for support, to the point where she had trouble keeping up with her schoolwork. At the time, I couldn't realize how this drained her. She enabled me to get a psychiatrist, Dr. Charles Richards, whom I started seeing in the spring. In spite of my drain on her, we remained good friends for many years. I never missed any classes, but did little home studying. She died several years ago after a fine career in the teaching of psychiatry to medical students. She'd had two mastectomies, did okay for a few years, then died of breast cancer.

In my regular physical exam that spring at med school, the doctor found a breast lump, but instead of telling me, he told Dr. Richards. He (Dr. Richards) asked me about it, not realizing I didn't know about it. When he discovered this, he was furious and went to find the one who told the wrong person. He was gone a long time and later I got an apology from the appropriate doctor. They arranged for me to have a breast biopsy. For that, I was hospitalized for two days. I was treated very well by everyone, which eased my anxiety.

There was confusion about the anesthesia. I requested only local because of my hatred of ether, but the morning of the surgery, they prepped me for a general anesthetic. An intern started an IV, running it very fast because as a medical student I "should be able" to tolerate the bladder pressure! I had a terrible need for the bathroom long before the IV finished. Then I told them I was not to have a general anesthesia and confusion reigned. But eventually I was given a local and operated on by Dr. Frank Glenn, a high-up surgeon on the staff, who very helpfully talked to me as he did the surgery. It was benign and recovery was uneventful.

I did okay on my exams. In June, I stayed on because I had obtained a summer job in the Physiology Department. All my other friends had gone. Dr. Richards was on vacation, and I felt worse and worse. I sat in my room with the window wide open. I began to fear I would jump from the window, so I couldn't go close it. Finally I went around the halls to find any student who might be still there. I found a senior woman, still there because her graduation was coming up. I knew Barbara slightly. She was asleep. So I left a "help me" note on her door. After a while she came, closed my window, and found out the problem. She then spent time and had supper with me, then arranged for hospitalization at Payne Whitney Clinic (the psychiatric part of New York Hospital).

I spent the first full day secluded and crying and learned the next morning they had planned to move me to the real "disturbed" floor, but in the morning I was able instead to be transferred to a "better" floor. I wrote a note to the physiology professor about the job I was supposed to be starting, but learned in the fall he never got it—I felt terrible about that.

Dr. Richards was not formally on the in-patient unit staff, so I was not allowed to see him. This was a major disappointment. I was assigned a resident, whom I didn't like, gave him a pretty full story but refused to tell him the worst. After a month, Dr. Richards was formally instated and saw me regularly. Just at that time, Frances had her first baby, Andra, and I was determined to go help her. After debating the issue with the doctors, they let me go for a few days, which helped my self-esteem. Fran said I really was a help to her, in spite of my being very anxious.

When classes began in the fall, I attended at first from the hospital, but after a few days moved back to my dorm room in the Nurses' Residence. I was much better. My classmates knew what I had been through, and both men and women welcomed me back with respect and support. It was a wonderful class for all four years.

The second year went pretty well, except for an embarrassing incident. I had done a research project with one male student. The presentation at the end involved my projecting a series of slides while he presented the paper to the class. When I turned on the projector, the fan made such a racket I couldn't hear him at all. I panicked and the whole box of slides fell on the floor. I picked them up and ran them, in random order, with no regard to what my partner was saying. Of course I felt helpless and foolish, but nobody said anything.

After that year I passed Part I of the New York State Boards, the pre-clinical part.

The Hospital for Crippled Children was rebuilt on the New York Hospital campus while I was in my second year and was renamed the Hospital for Special Surgery. I felt like I had come full circle!

Some time in the second semester of either this or the following year, Fran and Dave set up a blind date for me in Philadelphia, where they lived. We went to the man's apartment, where after a while he stretched out on a counter and had an erection which was very obvious. I ignored it, and after a while he took me back to Frances' house. That was the end of that. They arranged another date for me, with a man I liked. It didn't bloom either.

I continued seeing Dr. Richards weekly. At the end of the second year, I got a summer job as a psychiatric extern at Kings Park State Hospital on

Long Island. I went by train to Manhattan each week to see Dr. Richards. In my work, I did very well at Kings Park.

I met two men at Kings Park, who were there because they were conscientious objectors doing their alternative stints: Martin and Dave. They were very musical; Martin playing the violin and Dave the cello. They were trying to get a chamber group together and learned I had taken piano. They wanted me to play for them. After I tried to dissuade them, I finally agreed. It was a mess—I hadn't played for several years—and afterward they were happy to let me not play. We remained friends. Martin and I became very close, and after I returned to school for my third year, we continued to see each other. He took me several times to hear his chamber group play wonderful music in one of the players' apartments. I remember especially the beautiful *String Quintet (Op 163)* by Schubert. I was the only audience. Martin and I spent a lot of time together, becoming romantically involved.

In the fall, when I was home for Thanksgiving, Aunt Bessie had been there for some weeks, getting sicker. She slept in my bed and by the time I got there, she was bedridden. I stayed with her almost constantly. She was heavily jaundiced and was essentially unable to communicate. She declined slowly and died while I was still home, but I felt I didn't dare stay past the beginning of classes, so I believe I did not stay for her funeral. I was not aware of feeling any grief, but I was more withdrawn for a while.

Martin's stint was over by Christmas, and he planned to take a freight boat trip around the world, earning his way by playing violin and other ways. First, however, he invited me to go with him to visit his family in Kalamazoo, Michigan, for a few days at Christmas. I loved him dearly by then, but he told me that I wasn't the one for him. I was not really surprised, because based on my previous experiences, I didn't really expect any kind of commitment. On the drive there we got headaches and I believe the car was in such bad shape that we were getting carbon monoxide poisoning. Fortunately he got rid of the car in Kalamazoo. His family was very fine, and the visit was great, mostly because Martin and I spent all our time together.

I saw him off, and I returned home by plane, where my mother was getting sicker. When I had told her I was going with Martin for Christmas, she had said, "Maybe you should go." I tried to be nice to her, but my heart wasn't in it. It was her last Christmas.

I returned to school, where I went through various clinical rotations. One of them was Labor and Delivery, and while on that for two weeks students were required to live in what seemed like an attic made into very small bedrooms over the delivery rooms. We were on constant call. While there, a male friend visited me at my suggestion. I don't remember how I met him, but he was not a student. We had a pleasant time together but nothing memorable. I never saw him again.

Also while there, I got a hankering for cheese. In our cafeteria, we got little cheese, which I love. So I bought a large section of cheddar, took it to the room, and proceeded to eat it all. Shortly afterward I threw it up.

I enjoyed very much the delivery room. Under New York State law, we were required to deliver a certain number of babies (five or six?) to graduate. Generally it was rewarding to deliver and then see the mother and baby together. But one delivery I'll never forget. My student partner, Harry, was a fine man. We waited for the baby to descend, when suddenly it emerged in a burst and we saw immediately that it was anencephalic (small head—which is why it came so fast—and no brain). The caul was intact and had to be broken.

After everything was finished, I had to get some data from the mother, who was fighting back tears. How I wish I had taken that time to talk with her. I didn't. Harry and I went for coffee and talked about it. Harry was Catholic, and I asked him if God would have allowed us to euthanize the baby. He said that God would have him die in time; it was up to Him.

Another rotation was neurology, for which we went to Bellevue Hospital where Cornell had a neurology ward. We had to get down from 68th Street to lower Manhattan. Both hospitals were near the eastern shore of Manhattan, with the FDR Drive between them and the East River. Wearing our white coats, we would go in groups of two, three, or four, out to the Drive and hitchhike. We were always picked up quickly. The businessmen using the Drive knew who we were. We learned a lot at Bellevue. We must have returned the same way.

In Emergency I had a young man whose upper eyelid was cut in a fight. I sutured it very painstakingly and slowly. He was very patient and got a top-rate result. His eye was okay.

I had one "boy (man) experience." A male classmate took me walking in Central Park. I was conversing fairly well. He suddenly whirled around in front of me and pushed against me and had an orgasm. I know he was embarrassed, as was I. We couldn't talk about it.

Some time in my second or third year, a female student from the class behind us invited me out to a restaurant for her birthday dinner. Ann was somewhat of a loner and apparently wasn't comfortable with her own classmates and thought I was the most approachable. She suggested we have cocktails. Until then, I had never had an alcoholic drink, but my attitude had slowly tempered. Ann suggested I have a daiquiri, a good one to start with. Since then, I have enjoyed daiquiris and other types now and then.

In March, letters from home indicated Mom was worsening. I arranged for her to be admitted to New York Hospital. She was brought by the Chatham ambulance at no charge. Dad came separately. She was under the chief surgical resident's care, whom I admired.

Later on the day of her admission, I talked to friends at the dorm, who told me I was developing a rash! It was German measles. We all agreed I should be in the infirmary, so I went there. Someone told the surgeon and my mother. I told the nurse I was having leg cramps, and the same surgeon came to check me out, afraid it might be something like polio. He found it not so. He reported to me about my mother. Late that night he came again to tell me my mother was obstructed in her colon, which was no doubt from her cancer. Obstruction is an emergency, and they did surgery then, in the middle of the night. The surgeon came to me afterward (still night) and said she came through okay but the cancer was widespread in her abdomen, and his only choice was to do a colostomy (attaching the best end of the colon to an artificial opening in her abdomen). A few days later, after I was recovered from rubella, she went home by ambulance to die.

She hung on until I got home in June. She was in my bed, eating little, able to converse a little. One day she asked that Dad, Fran, David (Fran's husband, an attorney), and I gather around her bed. She gave us some instructions, especially to Dave. We assured her that it would all be done the way she wanted. I was feeling slightly "out of it" and hung back a little.

Fran had only a week or so before delivered her second baby, Deena. Both Andra and Deena, as well as Fran and Dave, were with us. They were using our parents' bedroom and feeling quite cramped. Taking care of a new baby in a strange place, among a lot of people, with so much emotion floating around, was very hard on Fran.

Mom lasted a week or so after that. I stayed with her constantly and used what had been Fran's room for myself. Before my arrival Dad, Aunt Muriel, Auntie Nan, and Aunt Jennie (Uncle Fletcher's wife, who had come to help) had cared for her in shifts. Frances was told on her arrival that she had a shift, which added to her stress. Once I was there they left it all to me. I felt deserted. I was not given instructions as Fran was about moistening her lips and giving her Demerol, and I didn't know what to do. Med school doesn't include nurse's training. At one point, after Mom was essentially unconscious, I thought how could this go on? I put a tourniquet on her arm to see if I could get a vein. I did not really expect to do anything, but her circulation had collapsed anyway. She died a few hours later, and I went to tell the others and to call her doctor and the funeral director. I felt depersonalized (out of it).

I returned to the school, where I had a job doing lab analyses. I called Dr. Richards from there. He said little. I developed a very painful torticollis and went to Student Health. The nurse there confused psychosomatic and malingering and gave my head a huge sudden whack to surprise me into releasing it. It hurt and I yelled but it didn't release. I left. It slowly relaxed over the next few days. I didn't want to be home, but returned for the funeral. During all the conferences that had to be done, I hung back and said little. Mom's body in the coffin was on display at the funeral home. I didn't like the way the funeral director had done her face. I guess he wanted her to look young and healthy instead of the truth, that she was sick and gaunt. He had filled out her cheeks and used rouge on them. She had never used make-up. To me that wasn't my mother, not the truth, but I never said anything. The funeral service was cut and dried; no eulogy in the Episcopal church. Then we had to ride a long time, more than an hour, to the cemetery in Brooklyn. Three or four generations of Dad's family were buried there.

Shortly after, I traveled to the University of Rochester, as I had a summer job as psychiatric extern. I learned a great deal, as they gave me the same responsibilities, studying and writing requirements, as an intern. Thorazine, the first working drug, was just coming out.

One of the newly admitted patients was a young mother who had just given birth and had a severe post-partum depression. I was strongly affected by her pleas to have her baby with her. (Today that would be encouraged.) I was close to tears and couldn't do my work. I went to the Chief Resident on the floor to ask how I could get myself through this. His name was Dr. Jim Bartlett, and I will never forget him. We talked, and together we figured out that I was feeling grief for my mother, and the mother patient triggered those feelings. As a result he referred me to a senior staff psychiatrist, with whom I had several interviews. But after that first talk, I was able to work. Jim continued into an illustrious career in the medical school as Dean, and in later years in the Middle East. However, whenever he was back or I saw him in the hall, he always had a friendly word for me. He died a few years ago of cancer.

Since Mom died, I had insisted on paying Dr. Richards something out of the tiny legacy she had left me. Before that Dr. Richards had seen me for free. I saw Dr. Guion a few times during the four years, and she was always supportive, even when I was depressed.

The fourth year was very full of more clinical rotations, including some direct patient work in psychiatry. I found I could empathize with my psychiatric patients quite well. The graduation was a very proud one, with Dad and two aunts present to see me get my M.D. There were seventy-six graduates in the class, same as in my high school class. I passed Part II of the State Boards.

I had applied for a two-year rotating internship at University of Rochester, which included six months each of psychiatry, pediatrics, surgery, and medicine, in that order. I had also applied for a one-year internship at Abington Hospital in Abington, near where Fran and Dave lived. They had a psychiatry department, but the internship included it for only one month, although that was more than most community hospitals offered. It was my first choice, but they turned me down, whereas the University of Rochester accepted me! Dr. Richards said the University of Rochester knew better than I did. I had to say goodbye to him.

INTERNSHIP AND MARRIAGE

ROCHESTER HAD SIX HOSPITALS: STRONG MEMORIAL HOSPITAL WAS AND IS THE main teaching hospital for the University of Rochester School of Medicine and Dentistry. Rochester General, Highland, Genesee, St. Mary's, and Park Ridge are the others. In Brockport is Brockport Memorial, where I did some work for Western Monroe CMHC (more on that later). Park Ridge was the newest built. Genesee shut down in 2000 for financial and political reasons.

I now really needed a car. David (my sister's husband) found a repossessed one, a 1947 green Plymouth two-door. Dad drove his panel delivery truck with my belongings and followed me up the Thruway to Rochester. I felt free as a bird and drove quite fast. Poor Dad; he said he had trouble keeping up with me. That car lasted me seven or eight months, until after I was married. It suddenly dropped its transmission in the middle of the street. After that I used my husband's car, as he bicycled to work.

I started off in psychiatry, living in the Staff House. The rotation was from July to December. Our cohort was two men and myself. They became good friends to me. By then, even in medical school, I was able to be good friends with men. Martin, of course, had played a major role in my growth. I enjoyed the psychiatric work. I was really beginning to feel comfortable with psychiatric patients. I was ahead of the other interns because of the previous year's externship and of my work at Kings Park the year before.

I made friends with one of the social workers, Marian Roberts. When I visited at her house, she introduced me to her friend, Brita Lilius. She (Brita) worked at Kodak as an artist and arranged a blind date for me to play badminton with a Wallace Rust, an engineer at Kodak. Our badminton was lousy, but we started dating regularly. He flew home to Erie, Pennsylvania, for his birthday, September 2. I picked him up at the airport on his return, which pleased him very much.

In the meantime I had also met a young man who was Asian-American. We dated a few times. Then he asked me to come to his apartment. I declined, saying I thought I would soon be engaged, and he cheerfully acknowledged my decision.

Wally lived at the YMCA and took me to his apartment there a number of times, and we went out for dinner and other outings. About a month or so after we met, we talked about my expectations of the internship. I told him that the next rotations would be much more time-consuming than psychiatry, and I didn't see how we could see each other very often. By that time I was very much in love, and I guess he was getting there. Anyway, he proposed to me then, and we went out to celebrate at Edwards Restaurant.

We started to make plans. We thought of April to be the wedding date, but when I phoned Dad, he asked if we could do it in March, because the April date would be the Easter weekend, and of course his business would be very busy. So we set it for March 9, 1957.

We enjoyed our time together very much. We started making arrangements together, but in January I started the pediatrics rotation, and indeed my time became very full. From then on he did most of the arranging. He took me to Erie to meet his family, who were delightful. His mother and I quickly bonded.

For the wedding, Dad would do all the flowers and bring them with him. Frances would be my "matron of honor" (she was pregnant with her third daughter, Aerie); Izzie and Mary J. would be bridesmaids, and Barry A., a resident in psychiatry whose Staff House room was near mine, would manage the reception. Wally learned about the Unitarian Church. Its stated Principles intrigued us both (See "my Spiritual Autobiography"). We met with the minister, and he agreed to some small changes to his usual ceremony.

Very quickly I ran into difficulties with pediatrics. I was at first on call every other night, which I couldn't handle, and consequently I missed a series of 7:00 A.M. classes. My cohorts were the same ones I'd had in psychiatry. I soon realized that they were much more competent than I in Pediatrics (the opposite from in Psychiatry) and I goofed on some important cases.

During the time leading up to the wedding, I was placed on nursery, because the chief wanted to make that time easy for me. Other times, my colleagues, whether they realized it or not, did things I couldn't, so I usually got off okay. One time though I ate lunch where I couldn't hear the pager, and on my return to the floor found out I had been paged for a seriously ill new infant. My colleague did get there and he did the important things. I was rightly reprimanded. Another time, after I was married and living in our apartment, I was driving to work knowing I had an infant very ill with meningitis waiting for me. I was stopped for speeding. I'm sure if I had told the officer why, he would have let me off. He did ask if I was on my way to surgery, to which I replied, "No." What a good opportunity to have told him the truth! I had to go to court. My fine was thirty dollars, which was the same as my monthly internship pay. I told that to the judge and he discounted the fine but not the charge. He lectured me. Again, I found my colleague had done the necessary things for the baby.

This baby belonged to a gypsy family, which was large and emotional. They started doing ritual dances outside the baby's room. The nurses persuaded them to do their thing outside the ward, in the hall and elevator lobby. We had to communicate with the father as I recall. He was the only English speaker. The baby survived after a serious struggle for her life.

One thing I realized while on that rotation was that I couldn't be objective about very sick children. I felt their illnesses personally. Another baby, about two, with beautiful curly red hair, was admitted during the night, seriously dehydrated, after driving from the Southern Tier of New York. It was too late—"her brain had been cooked," said the resident. I was very impacted about her tragedy.

I was very anxious about the wedding. I had asked Frances if I could wear her wedding gown (at that time I weighed 105) and she agreed. The worst thing that happened was that I forgot to bring the wedding gown to the church dressing room! Someone had to go back to the Staff House to get it, and it delayed the wedding about fifteen to twenty minutes. Otherwise it went off okay, with the help of my sister and friends. It was not a big wedding.

For our honeymoon we drove to Williamsburg, Virginia., for a week. It was a very enjoyable trip and time. It was warm and sunny. We returned to Rochester to snow and cold.

Returning to the hospital was painful. I was not doing well at all. One evening I was doing some tests in the lab, and when I left, I overheard and then saw the department chief and my resident talking in the hallway, the latter saying my personality was unsuitable for medicine. They were both embarrassed, but I said nothing. I got more depressed and at home cried and cried. Wally tried to empathize, not very successfully. I decided I'd have to leave the internship in June. When I talked to the department chief, he required that I have a psychiatric interview with Dr. Myrtle Pleune. I knew her a little. I convinced her that I was fearful of doing poorly also on surgery and medicine and couldn't continue. So I resigned, but for a year felt guilty as I left my whole intern cohort to have to do the work of three with only the two of them. One of the rare times I left something unfinished, but a major one.

At home I suggested that since I wouldn't be working the next year, that I become pregnant. Wally agreed, and I got pregnant very quickly.

Some time during that year I had passed Part III of the New York State Boards, thus being eligible for a New York State medical license, which I applied for and received.

Building a Family

DURING THE FIRST PREGNANCY I WAS VERY DEPRESSED BUT DID NOT GET TREATMENT. I ate ham, a craving I think. I gained forty pounds, but my obstetrician, Dr. Richard Fullerton, wasn't worried because I started the pregnancy twenty pounds underweight, at 105 pounds. Physically, otherwise, the pregnancy went okay.

In early July, Fran was expecting her third baby. I took a flight to Philadelphia which, based on what happened, I believe was unpressurized. I had terrible abdominal cramps, but didn't complain. I should have asked for oxygen. I was about six weeks pregnant, which is a critical period in formation of the central nervous system.

The visit with Fran and Dave was pleasant. I was able to help with all three babies, and Aerie, the new one, was adorable. They now lived in a house in Wyncote, a suburb of Philadelphia.

In October, we were visiting Sunnywoods. Sputnik had just been launched. Dad and I—and I think Wally—walked up the hill to the cemetery, where we could have a good view without much surrounding light. We saw it go across the sky! It was precisely at the time and place that had been predicted.

My due date was in February, but early in the morning on January 28 the "water broke." I was only slowly leaking, so I didn't think anything would come of it. Wally went to work, leaving the car for me. I called Dick (Dr. Fullerton), and he wanted me in right away: "Risk of infection." I called Wally. There was quite a lot of snow on the ground and it was snowing hard. I got the car out of the garage, but got stuck very quickly. So I got the chains out and was putting them on when Wally appeared. He must have run all the way home from Kodak, many blocks away. He put me in the car and finished the chains.

When I met Dick at the hospital (Strong Memorial), he started a Pitocin drip, which would induce labor. It started very soon, and I was in hard labor all day long. It was quite painful and exhausting. Wally stayed with me all day. After twelve hours, I told Dick I didn't think I could go on much more. He had me taken into the delivery room. The head was stuck and not descending. He decided to use forceps (low, I found out later, meaning he didn't have to get them in very high). I received ether, which initially gave me the "willies" because of the pounding hypnotic noise, but it was only a few minutes, and Alan Paul was born. He weighed six pound something, not too small to go home. I nursed him on the table.

He was taken to the nursery and I to my private room. We named him Alan Paul, a beautiful name, I thought. I designed and made several birth announcement cards, with "Unto us a son is born" and the music from *Messiah.*

When he was brought to me that night at 2:00 A.M. to nurse, he was very red and too tired to nurse. I knew he had been screaming for some time, wanting to be fed. The nurse denied that and said something like, "He slept hard." I was furious, but said nothing more. When I had the later babies, I was able to insist they stay with me for on demand feeding.

At another feeding, I noticed that milk came out through his nose. I called it to the pediatrician's attention, Dr. Ken Woodward, who had been Chief Resident when I worked there. I was very fond of him. He took the baby and passed a tube down his throat to be sure there was no obstruction. It all made me nervous, because I knew that symptom could also mean a nervous system problem.

At home, Alan seemed to progress normally at first. A few days later, Dad, Aunt Muriel, and Auntie Nan came to visit the baby. We had invited them, but I had not had any idea how stressful a visit would be at that time. They did nothing to help (none of them had been mothers!) and didn't know what to do. Auntie Nan said to me, "I bet you looked at his feet first thing!" Later, I thought how ironic was her comment about his feet—I thought head more likely.

I remember Alan sitting in his play chair rattling a string of colored disks strung in front of him and babbling. But he never made eye contact and when he smiled, it wasn't a social smile where he would look at one. At about two and a half months, we visited a friend of Wally, who exclaimed about how large his head was. I was continuing to feel very uneasy about him, and a couple days later took him to his pediatric appointment. Ken measured his head, which was at the 99th percentile. He tried to look in his eyes, and then he took Alan down to an ophthalmology professor, Dr. Albert Snell. He was gone a very long time, and when he came back, told me Alan was probably blind.

That was on a Thursday. On Saturday, I felt his fontanelle (the "soft spot"), which I had done frequently. This time it was bulging. That was really alarming. I called Ken and immediately took Alan in. Wally went too. At the hospital they diagnosed (although Ken and I had already thought about) hydrocephalus. He was seen by the top neurosurgeon, Dr. Joseph McDonald, and admitted then for shunt surgery on Monday. On the way home Wally talked about possible electronic ways of helping Alan see. I said nothing, because I knew there was going to be a lot worse news come Monday.

We were at the hospital Monday, waiting for results. Finally Dr. McDonald, bringing x-rays, came to find us. The x-ray showed a large empty space. Alan's brain was squeezed just under the scalp. So in fact it was anencephaly. In effect he had no brain, and a shunt would not do any good. Wally and I were devastated. The full name of the condition was hydranencephaly. We ran away to Howard Johnson's. Wally talked about getting pregnant again. I said little. Finally we contacted Ken, who had been looking for us. We talked about what to do with the baby. He gave me some medicine to dry my milk, which turned out to be unnecessary. It dried from the shock. With deep regret, we decided to institutionalize him. He was transferred to Monroe Community Hospital. Wally and I had to talk to a social worker about costs. Wally refused to pay anything. I sat there gritting my teeth. The outcome was that when a bed would open at the Newark State School for the Retarded (now Newark Developmental Center) Alan could be transferred there.

I was crushed. When telling Dad what happened, I said he could tell others, but requested he tell them not to contact me about it. This was a mistake, I realized when I did receive a beautiful letter from my cousin Carolyn. She empathized with my grief, but offered hope for our future without Alan. I was very moved by her letter and realized why grief should be shared. To help myself through it, I painted a picture of Alan from a photo.

In a month I was pregnant again. I continued to be depressed. I was offered a part-time job at the Psychiatric Therapeutic Nursery at Strong in September. I accepted thankfully. I examined all newly admitted children. I was able to do that okay and attended conferences. I remember many of those disturbed children well. One in particular was Calvin, who wouldn't leave his mother's arms without screaming. He was three years old. He had no speech. I examined him in his mother's arms. Many years later, I got to know him better.

I was very depressed and spent a lot of time talking to the Nursery Director, Dr. Sally Staub. She was a wonderful woman. Like I had done with Nancy in medical school, I took up much too much of her time. One time, I lay down in the ladies' rest room. After a while Dr. Pleune came in and said, "You know you shouldn't have gotten pregnant so soon." She thought she had told me this, but I knew it anyway. I thought, *Try telling that to Wally*, but said nothing. She said I should be in therapy, which I also knew.

That summer, when I was quite pregnant, Wally and I took an auto trip through New England. I wore a corsage he had given me—I forget what the occasion was—but before the day was up he asked me to take it off. I guess he worried about what people might think of a very pregnant woman wearing

Paula holding Linda

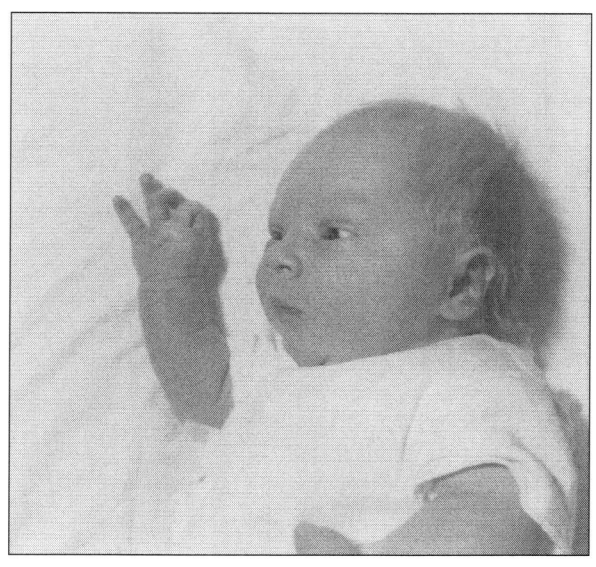

Alan

a corsage. We had dinner at a diner. I had a wonderful pork steak that could have been confused with a prime rib. The next day we were driving north. The car, with Wally driving, suddenly hit a gorgeous gold-orange cat running across the road. He was flung into underbrush beside the road. I wanted to stop and see if we could do anything for it and try to find the owner. I couldn't bring myself to speak up, and Wally gaily drove on. I felt sicker than I already had felt. That lovely cat has been on my conscience ever since.

We arrived in one city, I forget which, and finally found a motel down among the warehouses. We had brought hard-boiled eggs with us to snack on. We were walking among the warehouses after eating one, and I threw up alongside the sidewalk. We had thought boiled eggs would keep without refrigeration and were thus proved wrong. I woke early the next morning feeling sick and wanting breakfast. Wally woke enough to tell me I made too much noise (just dressing and sitting) and went back to sleep. I decided to go out to find food. I wandered quite a while without finding any place to eat. I felt miserable, but finally went back to our rooms. Even after dressing and driving, it took quite a long time for us to find food. Another nicer day, we set up our easels, and both of us painted a lovely scene with a covered bridge. I remember that trip with quite mixed feelings.

After getting home, I began to feel better. And in November, Wally and I drove to Wyncote to have Thanksgiving with Frances' family. I was feeling much better, and we had a thoroughly enjoyable visit. Even our sex was good. (Other than that time, Wally was very disappointed about my lack of enjoyment of sex, and in fact my resistance to it.) Wally and I were really happy at the time of that visit. Each pregnancy got worse physically, but not quite so bad emotionally.

Paula was born in the early morning of February 27 after an hour or so of relatively painless labor. She was a healthy baby, but I worried a lot about her. Once I was convinced she had a collapsed lung and took her into the emergency department where she was examined. Diagnosis: well baby, anxious mother, which was not an unusual diagnosis there. She also had a lot of loose stools and I was afraid she had celiac disease. (I knew too much!) When she learned to walk it was found she had slightly dislocated hips and had to wear a brace at night for many months. We also thought she was having "absence" spells, so she was on an anti-convulsant for several years.

Breast-feeding went well. I got involved with La Leche League, a support group for breast-feeding. I started to write a book for those mothers, and consulted a lot with Dr. Ruth Lawrence, who was a known expert. At the time she was breast-feeding her eighth or ninth child, while also being Chief of Pediatrics at Highland Hospital and a Professor at the medical school. She was very helpful. I wanted to do a questionnaire and asked a top doctor if I could contact the mothers from the Nursery. He refused. Foolishly I pressed my point, and finally he reluctantly agreed. Later I received a questionnaire in the mail that they sent interns, which I had not done because of depression. This time I realized they were pointing out the difficulties involved for the respondee. I responded immediately.

I sent out the breast-feeding questionnaire to one hundred or more mothers, scattered over the country, who I learned about. One sent back an empty one with an indignant note that she was too busy. Many came back, though, with interested and interesting comments. I incorporated much of this material in the book and planned to analyze them statistically. I wrote several chapters, but after Dr. Lawrence told someone it was a labor of love, I felt demeaned and lost interest. A lot of such books were coming out.

We had been told, regarding Alan, that the wait would be a year, and it was precisely a year when we were notified that a bed was available at Newark Developmental Center. Wally was not interested in participating. Paula rode in a carrier. We drove a Checker car at that time and could fit a porto-crib in the back seat. Alan would ride in that. I drove to MCH, did the papers with Paula in my arms, and picked up Alan. His head was definitely bigger and he was totally unresponsive. The aides on the floor were shocked that he was being taken. I had to carry both Paula and Alan to the car. Getting them into the car was a formidable task. The trip to Newark was long but uneventful. When I found out what building to deliver him to, an aide there said, in a loving tone, "Oh, he's a 'Big Head'."

After the nursery, I started doing camp physicals at the YWCA. One day I took Paula back with me to visit the Therapeutic Nursery. I ran into Dr. Pleune in the hallway. Paula responded to her immediately and reached up to her. Dr. Pleune picked her up, and I expressed amazement. Dr. P. said Paula sensed the bond I had with her (Dr. Pleune).

Wally and I decided to buy a house. We found one in Greece, a suburb, not far from Kodak. We moved in November, and at the end of December we had a terrific blizzard. Paula was ten months old. There was no electricity or heat for several days. The wind brought down lots of branches, so we had firewood and built fires. I opened the laundry chute door, right by the oven, and hoped some heat would go upward. There were no cars on the road. Wally stayed home. We got through it okay.

My dad brought us some raspberry bushes from Sunnywoods that I planted at the back of our back yard. They bore some raspberries, but neither Wally—because of the seeds—or Linda (our second daughter, see below)—because of allergy—could eat them.

Paula weaned herself from the breast at ten months but kept up a bedtime bottle for a year or more. She was doing well, though quite excitable and demanding.

We wanted a dog and went to the Humane Society. We picked out a large yellow German shepherd mix named Duke. We had built a fence around our back yard for him, but he immediately jumped over it. That meant we had to

Wally, Linda, Paula

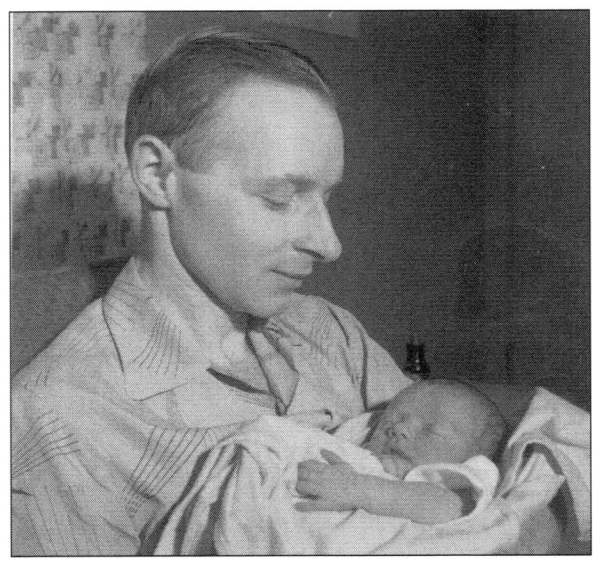

Wally holding Alan

Paula and Frances' four daughters — Andra, Aerie, Tara, Deena

run him twice a day. We went down to a ravine and woods, below Mrs. Garnish's house (she later became our babysitter). We could, for a while, let him run off the leash there. But after a few months, he became less and less reliable in returning to the leash, and meanwhile I had started my third pregnancy and was getting bigger. Furthermore, once when I wasn't paying enough attention, Duke attacked my friend Sally Staub as she came in the house. I was very upset by that. She wasn't hurt physically, but quite traumatized and I felt terrible about it. Wally and I decided we had to let Duke go. However he was very good with Paula, who loved him dearly. We found a farm family that already had several dogs who ran a lot and herded the cows. It sounded ideal, but I was concerned about Paula. She started crying when we left him. Wally distracted her, not realizing it would have been better to let her cry.

I had kept close contact with my friend Mary J. since college. She was now working for the CIA in Washington, D.C. In fact, she had visited and supported me while I was at Payne Whitney, although she did blame me for being depressed as I had "no reason to be." She visited our family while I was pregnant with my third child. I was very glad to see her. Later, after Linda was born, I talked to her by phone and tried to invite her for another visit, and she was being noncommittal. I got angry and dropped contact with her for then.

Wally and I joined the Rochester Memorial Society being established at our church. I was elected the first president for a two-year term. Such societies, groups who advocated for less expensive funerals, were being formed all over the country. The second year in April, I was quite pregnant with our third and we had just said goodbye to Duke. I and three other officers drove to Chicago for the first continental meeting. We were all four in very good humor and laughed a lot, especially in the car. When I got home, I found that Paula was no longer dry at night, as she had been for a few weeks. We had the babysitter, Mrs. Garnish, who lived down the street. She helped a lot while I was away. In June, Linda was born, also relatively painlessly. Paula was entranced by her, although coming so soon after my trip away and leaving Duke, her regression in wetting continued.

At home, I was busy with Paula, the house, and church activities, and then Linda. Finally when Alan was about three, I decided to visit him. I packed up the two babies into the car, Paula in the back seat in a seat belt, Linda in the carrier. It took a while to get the car ready with everything needed. It was a cold day. The drive to Newark was again long but uneventful. As we approached the main office, the Medical Director came out to meet us and announced that the whole hospital was in quarantine for hepatitis, didn't I know that? I was immediately disheartened. That whole trip for nothing. We drove home. Wally didn't even know we tried.

When Linda was a baby and Paula two and a half, I took them to a Family Week at Camp Unirondack (run by the Unitarian Church). Wally didn't want to go. He had a week's vacation and would work around the house. I took the car. At the camp, the adults had some wonderful discussions. I learned that a new hybrid corn would revolutionize feeding the starving third-world populations. Paula was well-cared for in her program, but I had some trouble caring for Linda while yet trying to attend adult events. But it was a wonderful week.

When we got home, Wally was waiting for us. He was ashen-faced and obviously ill. He had developed a urinary problem and had been in a lot of pain. Without the car, he had walked the several blocks to the nearest doctor's office. The doctor treated him, then drove him home himself. I had earlier unsuccessfully tried to persuade him to get his own doctor, but now he had one.

In the fall of 1962, I remember holding the children close and watching television at the time of the Missile Crisis with Cuba and Russia. What great relief it was to see it resolved peacefully. Kennedy was a great president. The next year in August, I heard Dr. Martin Luther King's "I Have a Dream" speech. I was—and still am whenever I hear it—very moved by it. Then in November, just before Thanksgiving, I was driving Paula home at noon from nursery school, and stopped at the church to deliver something for the Thanksgiving dinner. The minister, Dr. Williams, and another man ran outside and asked me if I had a car radio, that there was somebody saying the President was wounded. I didn't have a radio, and I raced to pick up Linda and then home as fast as I could, turned on the TV, and watched the whole horrible and memorable event unfold, watching with Wally, over the next four days, as the President's death and funeral played out.

Linda was a smart baby, as was Paula, but more docile than Paula. She completely weaned herself at nine months. A month later, I found she had a rash all over her back. Ken and I figured it was a food allergy and went about sleuthing it. To our surprise, it wasn't milk, but wheat! Wheat is very hard to eliminate, as it is in so many prepared foods. The rash disappeared but she later found she was allergic to other foods, especially to tomatoes, citrus, and watermelon, and suffered allergic rhinitis. For several years, she had desensitization shots. It's hard to say whether they helped, because the rhinitis has always been present in the morning.

I missed working and was becoming more depressed again. When Linda was one and Paula three, I entered Paula in a nursery school and arranged for more extended babysitting for Linda, then resumed the YWCA physicals. I found one very severe heart murmur and referred the mother to her pediatrician.

I was quite worried about Paula. She was very persistent and intense in everything she did. In some ways it was good. For her third birthday Wally and I gave her a tricycle in the morning. She rode it round and round the rooms, screaming the whole day, bumping into doorways and furniture. At the end of the day she had totally mastered it. On the other hand, one time the nursery school teacher told me Paula refused to tuck her scarf inside her jacket when playing outside because I didn't do it that way. When outside, that was dangerous. That was easily solved. They also told me that often she would sit in a corner and cut up paper into little pieces and insisted on keeping this up for long periods. One day in the winter after snowy driving, I was about to let her off at the nursery school when the teacher came out and reminded me today was a holiday. I burst into tears, and the teacher then insisted on keeping Paula for the morning.

I also found several friends whom I frequently visited in the mornings. One in particular I spent quite a lot of time with, as I had with others during previous depressions. She was a Nursery parent. Her husband was an economics professor at University of Rochester. He helped me with the statistics from my breast-feeding questionnaire for writing the book.

One incident occurred when Paula was about three and Linda one. They were both in the bathtub bathing. Paula suddenly defecated into the water. I was so furious I threw her across the bathroom floor. I realize in retrospect how my mother must have felt that time she almost beat me. I guess it can happen with most mothers, even those who are normal and not seriously abusive. Fortunately, Paula was not physically hurt, but I'm sure it was traumatizing to her.

Paula loved to talk at dinner about her day at nursery school. Her language and vocabulary were excellent. Wally thought she talked too much and one day at dinner reprimanded her quite harshly. Thereafter when she talked, she directed it specifically to me and mumbled it. She continued mumbling, especially when he was present, until she was out of high school.

As a family, we visited Wally's parents ("SID" for Sarah I. Durbin, and Al, though I called them Mother and Dad as Wally did) three or four times a year, usually on a weekend. The first few years Wally's paternal grandmother and his younger sister, Iola, were also there. Iola is twelve years younger than Wally. Not long after we were married, Iola "escaped" from her grandmother, whom she blamed for the unhappy home, by marrying and moving to Ohio. Some years later, the grandmother was hospitalized in the local community home. Thereafter, Wally's parents were happier. I remember their very celebratory fiftieth wedding anniversary, with cousins from all sides, and Iola, Don (Wally's brother), and Wally and spouses present in Al and Sid's basement, which took on the excitement of a party house.

Our visits always included cards, like poker, and word games, like Boggle, with Mother, Paula, Linda, and me in the kitchen at their dining table. Those games were so much fun; we laughed and laughed. All of us were positively challenged, especially by the word games. Mother was really a brilliant woman and very quick-witted. (She was a head cashier in a department store.) Wally and Dad would talk in the living room, over Dad's pipe. We would play till late in the evening. Mother was also a very good cook, and we enjoyed her meals. She made egg noodles from scratch—delicious! She cried every time when we left after visiting them.

One time I was driving the girls home in the Checker. It was raining and the streets were wet. The girls were buckled into the back seat. Linda (I think she started this) unbuckled her belt, whereupon Paula did too. I stopped the car at the side of the road, got out, and went back to buckle them in again. This happened another three or four times! Each time I went back and buckled them in. As we were going north on Dewey Avenue, there came a dip in the wet road right where the car in front of me stopped to turn left. The Checker slid forward in spite of my braking and hit the other car in the rear end. Both girls had just been buckled in again and none of us were injured. Linda had a bruise on her stomach, presumably from the belt. Someone called the police, who appeared quickly. The other car was drivable, but mine was not. The policeman took down all the data, called for a tow truck, and drove the girls and me home in his police car. I called Wally. We had only the one car; I don't remember how we managed the next few days without it. I'm all for seat belts!

I regret that my depression caused me to neglect providing music for the girls to listen to in their young years. The Toronto station wasn't reliable. I could have played records, but that felt like a hassle.

We bought a piano, which I had wanted for a long time, when Linda was four. Wally said I had been a good enough mother to now deserve it. The girls started lessons at the Hochstein Music School when Linda was four and Paula six. Hochstein is an endowed school for the community. They give a lot of scholarships to many inner city children and are open to all socio-economic groups.

Neither daughter took to it. I discovered that Paula's teacher had hit her hands with a ruler. I reported it and she was fired, but unfortunately it must have added to Paula's dislike of classical music. She will have nothing to do with it, except for that to which the children can dance. Linda is more musical; she usually sings in choruses wherever she lives.

I enrolled the girls at the YWCA for swimming, and the Hochstein School for music because I wanted them to become comfortable with a diverse group of children. They certainly didn't get that at their school. Both grew up to be very accepting of all people.

Louise Smith, a member of the Unitarian Church, and I founded a group with several other women, both black and white, to review children's books that demonstrated diversity among children. PARTNERS was a mnemonic for a wonderful name having to do with reading, children, and diversity, but for the life of me I can't remember it. In the move to New Jersey (see the last chapter) I had to get rid of many files and that must have been one of them. The other members of our group have deceased or I've lost contact with them, so there's no one to ask. During PARTNERS' existence, we tried to publicize it and went places and gave talks. It lasted several years. One mother had to drop out because her husband was an extreme conservative and didn't want her involved in anything like this. By the time it petered out, there were a lot of such books being recognized by many organizations.

I became quite busy at church, joining the choir and at times babysitting the nursery class during the Sunday service. Consequently Wally did quite a bit of babysitting, especially Sunday mornings and weekday evenings for my various meetings (La Leche League, Memorial Society, PARTNERS, choir rehearsal, etc.) Finally Wally got fed up and one Sunday as I was leaving for church, he scolded me quite roundly, and I cried all the way to church. When I got there my face was very red and the choir members were embarrassed by me. The next week I resigned from the choir.

Some time later, I joined the RE Committee, chaired by Ruth Coakley. A year or two later, I began to teach second graders. The curriculum was about emotions. I enjoyed preparing the lessons. They included stories, songs, puppets, and drama. Although the children didn't say or actually act much, I could tell they were "being" the characters. I heard a child psychiatrist say this course could be dangerous for the children. I thought, *This is true. What better person than myself to teach it?* There was one boy who was obsessed with eyes in his drawings. I saw that his mother had hyperophthalmos (bulging eyes) and asked her if she was under a doctor's care; she said yes. I didn't try to talk to the boy about it, which I knew would be unwise in that setting. All the children survived quite well.

In the third year of this, a photographer joined the class to make a documentary of the course. He was great, knowing just how to avoid eye contact or interaction with the children so as to get candid pictures of them going about their class, ignoring him. I wrote captions for the documentary, and at Ruth's suggestion presented it at a Unirondack RE Week. I was pleasantly surprised by the positive comments about it. I taught this course for three or four years, often driving to and from church with Ruth. We became good friends.

In looking for more part-time work, I found that Planned Parenthood needed a doctor, and a manager hired me. This resulted in a rift between the manager and current doctor, who wanted to hire an Ob-Gyn specialist to do pelvic exams. I attended a clinic with the doctor. Both of us realized how inappropriate my placement was and that was the end of that.

When Alan was five and a half years old I was at the YWCA, doing physicals while Paula and Linda were in the Tiny Tots swimming class. How they found me I don't know but I received a call from the NDC Medical Director that Alan had died, I don't know from what. I remembered that Dr. Snell, the ophthalmologist, had said he'd be interested in an autopsy, especially of his eyes. I instructed the funeral director to take him there (I was never charged), and Dr. Snell's office to have him cremated after the autopsy. I never heard from any of those people. Wally left it completely up to me. I never saw Alan again.

I think of him from time to time, especially on his birthday. Sometimes I used to mention it to Wally. But no discussion ensued. The girls knew the story when they were older, but of course they have no memory of him. Usually now I just think about him and how old he would be and that maybe he'd be a lawyer or something, but I keep it to myself.

In 1963, I started therapy with Dr. Pleune, against Wally's wishes. She saw me three times a week until 1968. The children grew well. When Linda was in nursery school, she went Tuesdays, Thursdays, and Fridays because that was when my therapy appointments were. She later told me it was confusing because the Friday children were not the same as the Tuesday and Thursday children. She took her own snack of rye crisp because of the wheat allergy. That was okay because she could share it with others. Paula was doing well in kindergarten.

Wally was very good at making and repairing things, and when I had a physical problem, he could be empathetic and helpful. One time when I was quite pregnant, I was insulted by a very young woman in a store. I told Wally about it, and he was quite angry. One time when pregnant I was severely constipated, and he was quite helpful then. He could take care of anything practical, and in emergencies was exemplary. He was also very compulsive and wanted everything perfect and done his way. For example I had to be sure the roll of toilet paper should be installed a certain direction and not try to use or save small soap pieces. He was angry if I left a project (e.g., pruning a bush) not cleaned up right away and could be very critical of my shortcomings. One time regarding a meal I made, he compared it unfavorably to his mother's cooking. That time I responded quite strongly to him, saying I was not his mother and he shouldn't compare us. She'd had forty-odd years of cooking, and I about two months' worth. He stopped. He was also very critical of Paula in many ways, especially in her teenage years. We had a major problem (i.e., impossible) in discussing emotional issues. Our relationship was quite mixed.

Beginning My Career

Late in 1964, when Paula was five and Linda three and a half, I decided to get a part-time job at Rochester State Hospital. Wally was against it; he thought I was too non-functional. I had known from the beginning that he was "anti-psychiatry," but I did it anyway. Paula was in kindergarten and Linda in nursery school. I arranged appointments with two of the hospital directors, but at the last minute Mrs. Garnish couldn't come. I called Dr. Pollack, and he said bring the kids anyway. I was a little apprehensive, but we took coloring books, etc. Dr. Pollack had a large office, so I sat the girls at the back with the crayons and the interview started. The girls were amazingly good. Once Linda quietly came up and asked me a simple question. I answered her, and she went right back to her spot. I was very proud of them, and Dr. Pollack was highly impressed. He had received reference letters from both the Psychiatry and Pediatrics Departments at Strong Memorial Hospital. The one from psychiatry was "excellent," he said. However the one from pediatrics he wouldn't quote, but implied it was pretty bad. Much later I was told by someone that they had heard Dr. Pollack say that, regarding me, whenever I walked into a room, my presence was palpable, or words to that effect. It was nice to hear that! I had the second interview, and I was hired to start January 2,1965, as Psychiatrist Grade I. I was told that being half-time I couldn't receive residency training.

I worked on the women's wards, both admission and secondary. I had many fascinating experiences and learned a great deal about psychoactive drugs ("chemotherapy"), which were now available for both schizophrenia and depression and about patients and in-hospital treatment. I also learned a lot from social workers and the regular staff conferences. My mentor on the secondary floor was Dr. Irene Peer, and on admissions Dr. Richard Steckel. I got to know Irene especially well. Both of them were very helpful to me.

I subscribed to *Science*, a very erudite magazine put out by the AAAS. I started attending week-long conferences of the AAAS (The American

Association for the Advancement of Science)—two or three—and then of the APA (American Psychiatric Association) almost annually. Once I ran into a medical school classmate, Bert Brown, who was at that time Director of the NIMH in Washington and we had a good conversation. I also attended many weekend or week-long workshops and symposia on various psychiatric topics. I especially got to enjoy the ones on Cape Cod.

In the fall of 1967, the new Director of the Hospital, Dr. Russell Barton, thought I deserved residency training so I could get my Boards. For two years I went weekly to Syracuse University where RSH's psych residents attended lectures, most of which material I already knew quite well. If I had been a resident at Strong (which I couldn't have done halftime) I would have had much more rigorous studies with much reading and group conferences. The Syracuse course also included live monitoring of an on-going psychotherapy with a male patient. I was chosen to be the therapist (to be watched by the class through a one-way window). I believe I was selected because my English was good: all the other residents in my cohort were foreign-born. I was very anxious about being on the spot like this, and I sweated buckets under my arms to the point where I tried wearing extra sponges! But I did receive kudos from the instructor supervising the psychotherapy. I was so thrilled by this that I drove home with manic-like feelings. My depression was a lot better then anyway, and I arranged termination with Dr. Pleune for spring 1968. She said I had more work to do, which was correct. But I convinced her.

When I was finished in Syracuse I started seeing my long-term patient from there at the RSH (now Rochester Psychiatric Center) and arranged supervision with a Strong psychiatrist I knew pretty well, Dr. Alex Braiman, by recording my interviews with my patient. I was quite anxious about being exposed like this, but Alex seemed to think I was doing okay and suggested I open a private practice. I was very surprised at this and took some time for it to sink in. I found an office building being built near my home and was their first renter. It was exciting to plan the office layout, buy furniture, and do all the necessary things. Wally helped some. I saw some art pieces at the Memorial Art Gallery by Carl Zollo, a well-known Rochester artist. I commissioned him to make one for my office. It's a beautiful metal 3-piece embossed gold and black. You can see Australia or the sea in it. I hung it behind my desk. In 1969 I started seeing four patients, including my long-term one.

I think that must have been when I decided, again, that I needed my own car, having always used Wally's car since my Plymouth dropped its transmission. I got a used Dart, and was pleased with it for several years. I also started my own bank account, but I had to pull strings to get it. At that time, it was still customary for banks to require couples to open one jointly and not allow a wife to have her own! I called a bank VIP downtown, and it got straightened out. I donated my first $1000 to Cornell to help a female med student.

To satisfy another Board requirement, I worked at Monroe Community Hospital on the neurology ward under Dr. Marvin Goldstein for six months. I got to like him well, and I learned a lot. One of my patients was a young mother and schoolteacher who'd had a massive stroke. It left her in a "locked-in syndrome," meaning she couldn't speak or move anything, but whose thinking mind was intact. She could only blink her eyes to communicate. I asked her once if she wanted to die. She indicated yes. Her condition had a profound effect on me, wanting to do something to help. Nothing was possible.

In 1970 RPC started making massive changes in organization so people from one geographic "catchment area" would be together. More importantly, the plan was to do better treatment so people could aim at discharge sooner. At the same time the community was starting Mental Health Centers that would not only treat out-patients but would also receive dischargees in well-planned intensive programs. It was a wonderful plan, and I wanted to be part of it. I was transferred to a unit that was being a pilot project for the new plan at the hospital. I stayed there several months, really enjoying the atmosphere and able to do better treatment. Then the whole hospital massively reorganized, and I was back on a new "secondary" unit, Unit C in an old but more workable building. Again, Dr. Peer was my chief. I got to know patients very well. Also I became good friends with the social worker on my team, Jim Sorrentino. He went on later to an illustrious career as head of the East House Corporation, a halfway house program which became large and organized throughout the community. Another person I got to know well was Dr. Richard Kepner, psychologist for Unit C. We no longer wore white coats. The attendants were also supposed to wear street clothes, but they weren't comfortable with that and went back to uniforms. The staff got to know each other very well, with exciting leadership from Dr. Peer.

It was during that time that I started thinking again about possibly being hypothyroid. I consulted an endocrinologist at Rochester General Hospital, who confirmed the diagnosis on the basis of my symptoms even though my blood tests were borderline. He said that he saw many like that, and that they responded to thyroid meds. I did start thyroid medication in 1972 and it did help the fatigue, but it didn't stop the depressions.

One time at RPC, a woman patient started choking to death and I was called. She was on the floor, cyanotic. A male nurse was working on her heart. I had not yet learned CPR, but I winged it, breathing into her mouth and getting up the food she was choking on. Breathing into her mouth was much wetter than I anticipated! We did successfully revive her. She was taken to the infirmary for observation for a while. I got kudos from the nurses. Very soon, CPR courses were arranged for all interested staff (I'm sure my nurse told the powers that be that I didn't know it) and I signed up. From then until I retired I retook CPR every few years, but never had to use it again—so far.

One of my private patients lived a long distance away and was always afraid she'd be snowbound or otherwise prevented from getting to me and persuaded me to give her an additional month's supply of meds. Unfortunately one of the meds was Valium, a "controlled drug," meaning I had to take certain steps in prescribing it because of its potentially causing addiction. One of the requirements was that she get only one month's worth at a time. So I was clearly in violation. A woman from the state government's Department of Health came and insisted on seeing certain of my files and wouldn't give a reason. That included this patient's and the records of some others also receiving Valium or a similar drug. I wanted to get my patients' permission to do this, although I knew this particular patient would be upset. The woman finally persuaded me to let her go ahead. She actually lied about her purpose, I realized later. I was very apprehensive about this process. I still didn't know why. She came several times to my office. Finally I guessed what it was all about and was "invited" to meet with her team at a state office downtown. It ended up with me getting a "reprimand" about my patient's meds. The others were okay, and the officials actually told me my treatment of her was good. (How can they say that after just looking at a record?)

During this period, I was one time on my way to my private office and somehow pinched my left ring finger, with the wedding and engagement rings on. Quickly the finger blew up to a major swelling, and the rings were cutting off circulation. I think I did do one or two appointments, then drove to Rochester General Hospital E.D. They had to cut the rings off, then the swelling went down. I took the rings to a jeweler's to be repaired. The next morning at Unit C, as the staff gathered, I told them what happened. The Head Nurse, Mary T., remarked that I was really more sentimental than she had thought and that she saw me as having very good mental health! Little did she know.

Another time I stopped at a store on my way to my office and locked myself out of the car. I had to walk back home (no cell phones then), got in somehow, called the barber whose place was next to my office, and asked him to tell the couple there to see me why I was late. He very graciously provided them with chairs in the hallway. I don't remember how I ultimately solved that, but I know I finally did get to see the couple.

Some time during these years, my medical school friend Nancy R. (the one who helped me so much my first medical school year) came to Rochester to give a talk. I arranged to meet her in her hotel room afterward. She had already had two mastectomies and was easily tired, so she was ready for bed. We had a very good conversation, and she commended me on my major improvement in mental health. That was a nice boost.

Regarding my private office, Dr. Kepner (Dick) wanted to open a practice too in the late 1970s. He arranged to rent my office certain evenings. This worked out pretty well for several years, until I moved my practice downtown (see "Crucial Changes").

I took a mail order course preparing for the Boards and also built a brain with clay and pipe cleaners, both in identifying colors, from a workbook I had from medical school. After the required time for "experience," I was ready in 1974 to take the Psychiatry/Neurology Boards. I took the written part first. I went to Chicago for the second oral part. In the line for registration, I met a woman from Jenkintown, where Frances' family lived, named Dr. Betsy *Webb*! My live patient to be examined was a pleasant man with chronic schizophrenia. After the interview, I was questioned by two VIP psychiatrists. I was able to expound on a theory I had about long-term movement disorders in people after long treatment with phenothyazines (e.g., Thorazine). I think the examiners were impressed. I passed the Boards! I could now say I was a "real" psychiatrist and received a framed diploma to display in my office.

Growing the Family

Linda had an adventure her first afternoon in kindergarten. Going to school, she got on the bus, like we had talked about. She was to return on the same bus Paula did. Paula was in second grade. I stood waiting for them to get off the bus. Paula ran to me quite distressed, saying Linda was not on the bus. I was alarmed too, but told Paula we'd find her quickly. I called the school office and was told she was right there. The story was that she went out to the street instead of getting on the bus and started walking away in the wrong direction. Luckily our neighbor, Susan Nowak, who was a sixth grade "safety," keeping her post where the walk to the school met the sidewalk, saw Linda going the wrong direction, recognized her, and knew she should have been on a bus. Susan took her to the office. Paula and I drove there and got her. I sent Susan a thank you note. I shall always remember her sharp wits with gratitude.

Paula was still taking an anti-convulsant because when she was three or four she was apparently having "absence" spells, when she would appear "out of it" for a few seconds. When she was in second grade, I mistakenly allowed her access to the bottle because I thought she understood the schedule for taking it. Mrs. Garnish called my attention to Paula's incoordination a few days later, due to too much medicine. I took it away, stopped her taking it, and called Dr. Woodward. He said first that I shouldn't have stopped it abruptly, but then to leave it out and see if there were any more spells. She never had more.

School went well for both girls. I took part in some of the parents' activities, especially a planning project with some other parents, called Redesign. We took it seriously and made a report. But, as happens to many plans that are asked for so as to "involve the parents," it came to naught.

Linda was very compassionate toward animals of any type from very early on. When she was in probably second grade, she left for school one morning. Our neighbor had shot a skunk the night before. Linda came back to our door, crying and carrying the dead skunk in her arms. I commiserated with her, and said we would give the skunk a decent burial, but for now to lay it in the garage. She accepted this and went off to school with tears on her cheeks. I don't remember the burial, but we brought the event to a comfortable conclusion when she and Paula got home.

In the sixties and seventies, Cornell initiated CAU (Cornell Alumni University), a summer two to four week program of learning and relaxing: two lectures a day for five days. I went to the very first week with my children, who were pre-schoolers at that time. They had their own program which kept them busy most of the daytime. Wally was not interested and never went.

All in all, it was a real vacation on a beautiful campus. Although I was an alumna of Cornell Medical College, located in New York City, I had never seen the Ithaca campus. We stayed in a modern dorm with good facilities.

I remember the first set of lectures, given by Dr. Eisner, a wonderful speaker and a biologist. He talked about genetics, recently made newsworthy by the discovery of DNA. There were also political, economic, and social topics. I took one course on science fiction, which was fascinating. I enjoyed the stimulation/respite ratio thoroughly.

The three of us attended every year for about ten years. The most memorable event was in July 1969, when the assemblage gathered around the one TV in the dorm lounge at eleven o'clock at night to watch the landing on the moon. I kept Paula up to see it—she was ten—but left Linda sound asleep—she was eight. I tried to help Paula understand why this was so momentous. I have never forgotten the images on the TV or Neil Armstrong's words, and I felt enormous pride in the accomplishments of science.

CAU began to include bird-watching programs in the early seventies just as I was reawakening my interest in birds. Field trips started at 6:00 A.M., with the most knowledgeable and fun-loving staff of the Laboratory of Ornithology. The first group included a woman who kept us laughing during the car trips, but with difficulty harnessed her mouth during the bird walks. We also had lectures and demonstrations about birds. I really picked up my childhood interest in birds and at home started to go on bird walks, both by myself and ones organized by the Rochester Birding Association, which I joined. They also had monthly meetings, the program for which was often slides of someone's trip to some birding mecca. Later, Lou (see next chapter) and I went on a Nature Discoveries tour to Point Pelee in Lake Superior in Canada, north of Michigan, one of the best-known birding sites.

The Laboratory of Ornithology at Cornell was an intriguing place for window viewers, for they had many species that came close for the food, but the field trips, for which I had been given a wonderful pair of binoculars, were the highlights. We visited several kinds of terrain to see different varieties of species—water, especially along shorelines; woods; wetlands; and a big area of muck and high grass, a bog, which is too dangerous to enter (I forget its full name). A grasshopper sparrow was singing there but couldn't be seen. One time, right outside my window at the dorm, I saw a goldfinch flying in a vertical circle around a bush. It flew round and round, probably in a courting dance (goldfinches have several reproductive cycles every year). It was wonderful! I was especially interested in recognizing individual songs. I learned a lot about an immense number of varieties.

Peter Paul Kellogg, Director of the Laboratory of Ornithology, was in his nineties. He was exceptional as a teacher and bird-finder and amazingly agile in the most complicated terrain.

At home, I began going out alone more. Wally helped me make a reflective parabola (like the shape of a satellite dish) which could focus bird songs at a spot in front of its center. Then a microphone was attached (supported by a brace of wires) to this focus and connected to a tape recorder. That way I was able to record some songs. I also had a fairly large collection of recordings made by the Laboratory of Ornithology and other sources. Once I saw an Eastern bluebird; I saw numerous goldfinches and other less common species. We kept feeders full in our backyard.

In the eighties, after I met Lou (see "Crucial Changes" for more on her), and after the children were old enough for summer jobs, Lou and I attended CAU together, several times doing the bird-watching seminars.

The energy required for the hiking and walking began to get me and Lou to a lesser extent. Also, the campus itself, as beautiful and varied as it was, and although there were circulating buses, still required a lot of walking. So we stopped going in the mid-eighties, and started signing up for trips and cruises. But I have retained my interest in birds, and in my bird book are notations with the many many species I saw.

Wally and I felt the girls should have pets. We bought a guinea pig for Paula. She was a light gold color. Wally named her Happy, hoping Paula would be happier because of it. She was lovely, and Paula took her to heart readily. Wally built a wonderful cage with sections. Then we bought Autumn for Linda, a lovely bronze color. The third one was also Linda's. She named him Feather because he was all white. They were favorites for several years, but they don't have a long life span.

When Paula was eight, her intensity and persistence again was obvious. She was wearing braids and wanted to do them herself. While Wally and I were eating breakfast, we could hear Paula screaming with each trial. If the braids were not perfect and symmetrical, she would scream while taking them out and start all over again. Intervention never helped. The best way was to let her scream until she was satisfied, which would eventually happen.

Paula got chickenpox. On the second and third days she itched terribly. She stayed with Mrs. Garnish, who didn't mind. She (Mrs. G.) must have previously had it. Wally came home on the third day and observed how badly she was itching. The next morning she was better, but he argued with me, finally "ordering" me to stay home. This struck me as anachronistic. Paula was better and was okay about staying with Mrs. Garnish. "Obey" was exactly the word that we had taken out of the wedding ceremony, and his job was certainly no more vital than mine, probably much less so. I stayed home, and did some typing.

At the church, I was invited to review the book *The Feminine Mystique* by Betty Friedan for a book discussion group. I was terribly nervous before getting to the church, unsure what dress to wear, and because I thought I was late, took a different from usual route, which turned out to actually take longer. But I did get there in time, and once I got there and started my presentation, I really did very well. It started good discussion and started me focusing attention on the Women's Movement.

After the guinea pigs were gone, we bought the girls gerbils, which had litter after litter. Wally and the girls built an apartment house for them out of plastic waste baskets turned on their sides, with screen in front. The girls spent hours playing with them. Paula especially kept track of their genealogy and all were named. One had broken a leg and it healed crooked. He was named Footsie. He was an adventurer. He would get loose in the house sometimes, and we thought he was leading others astray too. We would find him and sometimes others in a closet under some scarves, etc. One died, and I held Paula a long time while she grieved.

At ten, Paula was still wetting the bed. In the fall of her fifth grade we bought one of those alarms that sounds when wet. We explained it all to Paula. The first night it finally sounded as we were all getting up in the morning. It turned out that the wetting occurred just before she woke up. We placed the alarm for a few more nights, but it was never again needed.

A few weeks later, shortly before Christmas, Wally and I were downstairs after the girls were in bed. We heard Paula get up to go to the bathroom, then no sound. Wally concluded she was "eavesdropping" at the head of the stairs. He wound himself up into a major fury and ran upstairs to confront her. I ran after him, afraid he would beat her, and told Paula into her ear to go into a back room, close the door, and wait for me, which she did. Wally cooled down and went downstairs. After a bit, I went for Paula, talked with her briefly, and put her to bed.

We were then into Christmas vacation. On the morning of the girls' first day back to school, Wally left for his carpool to go to work while Paula was still upstairs without saying goodbye to her. When she realized he was gone, she ran through the house screaming his name. After a few minutes of this, I called him at work, telling him what happened and asking him to speak to her. They did talk and she calmed down.

A few weeks into the second semester, I discovered she was seeing "shapes" in her peripheral vision. She was also showing other signs of being stressed, such as every day rushing in the morning to see how fast she could open the orange juice and prepare it and get my timing of it. I was getting quite concerned and made an appointment with the community's best child psychiatrist, Dr. Werner Halpern. He listened very compassionately. He felt that family therapy was indicated. He wouldn't see her without the rest of us though. I knew Wally would refuse to do this. Then I appealed to the school psychologist, who made time in her schedule to meet with Paula weekly for supportive therapy. I'm very grateful to her. Paula gradually relaxed a little. After school was over in June, we went as a family to Washington, D.C. It was an okay trip with some strain, but Paula did okay. Later that summer she and Linda went to Camp Unirondack. Both had a good time there, and Paula came back refreshed. It had been not a good year. They went to Unirondack for several summers, where Paula picked wild blueberries.

A friend of Wally (Ray Newell) gave Wally a Monarch chrysalis on a milkweed branch. We set it up in the girls' bedroom and watched it. Wally set up the camera to take time release pictures. After several days it started to change from an opaque green color, becoming more transparent and light blue. Soon we could actually see the butterfly curled up inside the membrane. The process was slow and unhurried, until he was ready to break out. That happened suddenly during the night. When we all awoke we saw a beautiful Monarch clinging to the stem, flapping its wings to dry them off. When he was ready to fly, we opened a window, and set him free. It would be wrong to try to keep it. The girls were fascinated and had watched it closely, but do not remember it.

Some time in the early sixties, I think after Aunt Gladys' death, it became clear to me that our family has a genetic predisposition to breast cancer. On one of my visits to Chatham, I took with me a film on breast self-examination. I arranged a family (women) meeting to show the film and be sure all of us understood the risk. Not all attended, but my prediction has been borne out. In 1998 I had myself genetically tested, and it was, surprisingly, negative. However, two genes were known then to mutate (thus increasingly leading to breast cancer), but since then a third mutating gene relating to it has been found. Testing for it, the last time I asked, is not available yet.

Both girls did very well in high school. Some nights Paula and I talked late about how things were going at school. In 1977 Linda changed her name to Lynn and she has been known as such since. One summer Paula worked at Kodak in a dark room and saved a good deal of money. Two years later Lynn missed her chance to work at Kodak. Both girls worked summers and weekends at a nursing home, where they learned a lot about nursing homes and earned quite a bit, saving most of it. Both knew I was saving as much as I could for their college because Wally had long ago said he wouldn't pay for it. He also refused to submit a financial report which might have enabled them to get scholarships.

Paula and Lynn both declined nomination to the Honor Society because "it was too elitist." For several years in a row, Lynn seemed to be cheated out of summer activities that Paula did have, such as the Kodak job. One summer Paula attended a wonderful science camp, but two years later it had disbanded. Lynn had to attend a day field trip camp, with which there was too much bus travel and not enough good time. I was sorry we sent her.

I was having trouble with my neck. Later x-rays showed arthritis there and in my upper back, I suspect because of the difference in leg length. I consulted a physiatrist at Rochester General, who recommended physical therapy, in this case neck stretching. I went there weekly and bought a type of the equipment to use at home. The stretching did help. I was very sensitive to any slight breeze on my neck, especially in the car.

One Saturday morning I woke with crushing chest pain, referring to my chin, a clear heart attack signal. I went at once to Dr. Penna, who did an EKG, which was normal. On exam, he found my gall bladder was causing the pain. Some months later, he did make a cardiology referral and as a result I took a beta-blocker for a year. At year's end, the cardiologist tried to have me do a stress test. This time he ran the treadmill much faster. I couldn't run and panicked. The cardiologist apparently thought I was malingering or something, abruptly discontinued the test and beta-blocker, and dismissed me as "normal." Why couldn't I run? I think it was forecasting Parkinson's disease. After the move to East Brunswick, I received a "dobutamine" stress test, using injected medicine instead of a treadmill. It was normal.

When Paula applied to colleges, her first choice was Oberlin, partly because a boyfriend a year ahead of her was going there. Planning for spring break, she wanted to spend the week in Oberlin. Both Wally and I were opposed to this. I gave her an offer she couldn't refuse: to go to Mexico City where she had a pen pal. She, Linda, and I went.

We stayed in a hotel and took day trips to exotic places. We visited the pen pal, whose family was very hospitable and took us places. One was after midnight to watch and hear street bands called mariachi bands. Dick Kepner's parents lived there too, and his mother also met and took us to one of the museums. Lynn and I were careful about food and drinking water, Paula was less so. But it was Lynn who got the "Montezuma's Revenge" and was sick for a day. All in all it was a very good trip, except for that.

I taught Paula to drive. The lessons worked well, without any car mishap, but one day I wanted to sit on the lawn while she drove the car back and forth on the driveway. Wally was starting to mow the lawn. I tried to ask him to mow a little square jutting out from the lawn, so I could sit there without either of us disturbing the other for a while. He misunderstood me, thinking I wanted him to reverse his direction around the lawn. He started the mower, and I shouted to him over the mower sound. He worked himself into such a fury that he left the mower running and came across the lawn to me, knocked me down on the drive, and as I was in a crouched position, he proceeded to slap my face back and forth with his hands.

He had previously shown this sadistic streak a few other times. There was that incident when Paula was in fifth grade. Later, sitting in the dining room while Paula showered, he thought from the sound that she was running the shower too strongly. He started down to the basement. I asked him what he was going to do. He said he would turn off the hot water so the shower would suddenly go cold. He stopped and came up again. Another time when we were visiting his parents in Erie, a young neighbor boy kept intruding into our activities. Wally picked him up by the scruff of his neck and carried him back to his yard. Wally's father was quite shocked.

This last time, I thought, *This is the last straw*. I started thinking about separating. He went down to the basement. In a while I went in, having ended Paula's lesson, and he said, "Let's go on and forget it." No apology. He never could apologize for anything. I said nothing.

Paula graduated from high school in 1977, Lynn in 1979. Paula was accepted by Oberlin, and was co-Valedictorian with her best friend, Janet Bayer, out of a class of 388. She did not have to do a speech. They sang, "I Did It My Way."

When Lynn was sixteen, I started to teach her to drive. I had done well with Paula, but with Lynn I felt incompetent. She ran into a fire hydrant in the school parking lot. We didn't continue the lessons. So she didn't learn till several years later, attending a driving school.

Lynn decided to take her last semester of high school at SUNY Brockport. She needed only an English credit, for which she took British Literature, an excellent course, to transfer to high school records. In Brockport she also took pre-calculus, world history, and anthropology, but she says these courses were not challenging or worse. However, to the college she was very well prepared. Lynn was number ten in her high school class, about the same size as Paula's class. She had been accepted at Mount Holyoke College.

DECADE OF CRUCIAL CHANGES

In 1979-82, I made changes in every area of my life and the lives of my husband and daughters also changed. In the ensuing years there were more and more changes.

When the girls graduated from high school, they and Wally presented me with a beautiful black swan sculpture "for being their mother." I treasure it.

In November 1979, Rochester Psychiatric Center again reorganized. All my patients were gone, many discharged, and I was assigned to do annual physicals on a geriatric floor. This was not a way to advance my career. I saw by chance a small notice in the paper about the formation of the Western Monroe Mental Health Center in Greece, where my home was.

There were two other community mental health centers in the Rochester area. The goal was to have a center in each quadrant of the area, associated with a particular hospital with a psych unit. A few months later the fourth would be opened. It was largely due to a state pilot grant, a follow-through from the "catchment area" plan at RPC. What I knew of the plan, Integrated Mental Health (IMH), was good, that patients could live outside the hospital in group homes or halfway houses, both of which were being developed, and attend daily programs structured for their level of illness. Also outpatients of all kinds could receive psychotherapy, medicines, and when appropriate, Day Treatment. Right away I thought, I want to work there.

I had an interview with the Director, Beth Struever, ACSW, at Park Ridge Hospital, the sponsor of this CMHC. She was basically building this center single-handedly and chose a number of super therapists and clerical staff. There was already an operating office in Brockport, out at the western edge of the area. We liked each other immediately, and she hired me to be, at first, a psychiatrist at the Brockport office. I expected to start on January 2, but she and Dr. Mark Klein, Medical Director, persuaded me to start in December because they were already so busy. A new office building was almost ready to be occupied in Greece, and I would work there four days and at Brockport one day a week. I agreed to half-time, as I had been doing at RPC, but two things changed that: Paula and Lynn were now in college, and it turned out that I was most needed at the Center toward the end of the day. I continued my private practice.

Shortly before I actually started, I attended a weekend workshop on leading teams. In one session I attended, Dr. Mark Klein, the Medical Director mentioned above, participated, among others. We got to discussing my concern about my often being "teacher's pet," and wanted to avoid it in this next job if I could. Mark was favorably impressed with my comments, and I'm fairly sure he talked to Beth Struever about it. Of course I didn't avoid becoming "teacher's pet."

I resigned from RPC, and they gave me a farewell dinner. Wally came to it, as he had for other RPC dinners. He and Dr. Peer always hit it off well.

In January, I was driving to my new job on snowy roads, turned left, and was hit by a car coming toward me, I think too fast. It was a shock, and I felt dazed for a while. The car was somewhat damaged but my only injury was that my sternum (breastbone) felt bruised and possibly fractured (possibly by the shoulder belt). The other driver was not hurt. My car was drivable. I went to Park Ridge and called Beth. She arrived at the Emergency Department soon after I did and stayed with me, providing helpful support. I was examined and found bruised only. So much for not becoming teacher's pet. Beth thought my unconscious was punishing me for being finally professionally successful! I think she was right.

I enjoyed the job immensely, and it was a pleasure to work with Beth and supervise the therapists. Mark found he couldn't put in so much time and resigned. Beth appointed me Medical Director! Thereafter I participated in meetings there and also the Board meetings at the hospital monthly. I was privy to what was going on and at the Board meetings I gave a report, often a case history which had particular factors. The only doctor in the meeting was the Hospital Director, who often didn't come. My reports were meant to be educational in mental health matters for the Board members.

Later I attended a several-day conference on team management in Albany and felt very executive-like! At that time my arthritis was beginning to bother me, and I was taking aspirin four times a day, until my stomach rebelled, quite painfully. The new anti-inflammatories had not yet come out. I began drinking coffee excessively, because I could get it easily at work. My secretary brought it to me without being asked. I went to New York City for a conference and while there met with Fran and Dave, "for coffee." I noticed my heart beating with a lot of skipped beats. On my return to Rochester I wore a cardiac monitor for a day, but realized while wearing it that coffee was the problem. Reducing it helped a lot.

I had recently met a schoolteacher named Lou Gage. We became very close, and she was destined to play a very important role in the next part of my life. She lived and taught fourth/fifth grade in Spencerport, a town near Greece. She was a blond woman, trim and very attractive, who was close to my age.

• • •

Lou and Me and Western Monroe: Lou supported my wish to separate from Wally (which had grown gradually stronger since the incident out on the driveway) because of the other incidents with Paula, and his criticalness and need to control me and having to always be right, which had gradually become more demoralizing since our first year. In January 1981, I told him I was leaving. I hadn't thought far ahead and was thinking of only an informal separation. I said neither of us was happy. He was at first angry, saying he would go for a divorce, nothing less, which was okay by me. Paula was home for that month. I thought her presence would make the transition easier. It did for me but not for him. I had previously told each girl my plans, and both had wondered why I didn't do it before. My thought was I wanted to do it after the girls had started college. It would mean less moving hassle and possibly would be less upsetting for the girls since they wouldn't be there for most of the process. It also meant no custody battle. One Saturday morning after Wally had gotten up and I was still in bed, I heard him sobbing loudly downstairs. Otherwise he never showed signs of sadness, only anger.

I found a nice apartment nearer Western Monroe and moved out toward the end of January, after Paula had gone. Wally was surprised I did it so quickly. Lou helped me immensely, not so much with the actual move (she was teaching), but in the process of getting settled. We often had dinner together, and she often made dinner at the apartment for us. She gave me her extra pull-out bed.

I was very unhappy about all of this, even though I wanted it. I felt guilty for Wally and sad about the loss of my marriage. I started gaining weight, probably due to stress, after my weight had been stable at 125 since my pregnancies. As I had done before, I leaned too much on Beth, and she recommended I see her psychologist friend, Joyce DuBrin. I started with her in January. She saw me weekly. That next summer I participated in a weekend retreat and marathon where, in groups, everyone had plenty of opportunity to "work" on their problems. It was a memorable and very moving experience, and over the next years I participated in several more. A few months later she had me join a therapy group run by her and her husband, Bob Pierce, also a psychologist. I worked with her for ten years.

Some years later I went to a marathon week that Beth Struever was connected to, at one of the great camps in the Adirondacks, Sagamore. That was also very fruitful.

At Western Monroe my job was going well. Beth was still hiring therapists, and I was getting to know them. I did some of the interviewing. In Brockport, one of the therapists, Martha T., discovered she had a brain tumor and had to have surgery. Beth told her she would have her job whenever she could return. It was a neuroma, a benign, easily removable one. It left her deaf in one ear, but otherwise totally intact. She returned to work a few months later.

I remember interviewing Mary Garber in Greece. We found we had many interests in common. We later became good friends. I did several in-services for all the therapists, particularly on the mental status examination. These in-services went over well. On both the therapist and administrative staffs, I was working with men as well as women, and it was no problem. I was anxious about giving my Board reports, but on the whole they were okay. I could answer questions extemporaneously more easily than I could do my prepared report. Speaking extemporaneously made me focus on the person who asked the question rather than on my notes. I think that's why it went better.

Beth thought I should wear better clothes, which had always been a "bugaboo" for me, ever since my childhood without decent clothes. Shopping for clothes was quite traumatizing. If I spent any time at it, I would get depersonalized, meaning I would start feeling numb and unable to make decisions and felt like a stuck robot. I actually cried during this interview with Beth. She suggested that I ask Lou to help me. Lou accepted the charge readily. She was excellent in all matters of taste and grooming. She helped me shop and did a great deal for me. She gave me permanents, colored my hair, helped me with make-up, and much more.

Lou was a talented poet, writer, seamstress, and artist, as well as a fabulous person, kind and thoughtful, a lover of children and animals. I have many items she made for and gave me: poems; clothes; and paintings. After she retired from school in 1987 she went back to serious acrylic painting. She exhibited with the Greece Arts Group and sold several paintings.

She also suffered from asthma, which gradually got worse over the years.

I held a brunch at my apartment for the Western Monroe staff, including clerical. Lou prepared and managed the food. It went well. I had on display the clay and pipe cleaner brain I had made while preparing for the Boards. It was taking up space and attracted no interest. After that one exhibit, I felt I could then throw it away.

Lou and I decided to buy a house and live together. In May of 1982, we found a beautiful brick ranch house, for sale by owner, not even listed. We were so pleased. It had four blooming crabapple trees in the front. The back yard closest to the house was grass, garden, and bird feeders. Beyond that was a drop-off, terraced, with a path going diagonally downward through woods and poison ivy. Beyond that, just beyond our lot line, was a huge meadow belonging to our neighbor and a stream of water. It was a beautiful view. We bought it. Lou, mostly by herself, did major renovations. She moved in, but I waited until the improvements were nearly complete, in the fall of 1982. I didn't think I could handle the dust and disorganization. Beth and other members of the staff helped me move, and we had an informal lawn party afterward. I had forgotten about my raspberry bushes from Dad. Later I learned that Wally tore them out and gave them to Ray Newell, a friend. I resented that he had not consulted me.

Soon I hired a secretary to do my Medicare and Medicaid accounts. It was Pat Standhart, with whom I became good friends. She came to our house every Saturday morning until I retired, when she and her husband moved to Michigan. They sometime later moved back to the Rochester area. I've kept in touch with her.

One day in winter I was driving home from Western Monroe. Long Pond Road, which passes in front of Park Ridge Hospital, is very steep going uphill, and was solid ice. Halfway up the hill, I saw a car coming down in the opposite lane, spin out of control, cross over directly at me, and hit my car and several others coming up behind me. Finally near the bottom of the hill I saw a heavy truck turn sideways so the out-of-control car would hit him broadside and stop. I was driving my brand new Mazda then. It was damaged but drivable. I wasn't hurt, and I don't think the cars behind suffered any more damage than I did. But I worried about the driver of the out-of-control car. It must have been quite traumatizing to go through that and then strike the truck head-on. I hoped he had his seat belt on.

In May of 1984, Lou's and my house was broken into. My jewelry box was taken. The biggest loss was my engagement ring, my mother's engagement ring, and my wedding ring, with its inscription. I had planned to give each of the diamond rings to my daughters. I lost a precious heart-shaped locket in which I had painstakingly inserted on one side a small picture of both girls and on the other, one of Lou. That event created a big void in me. Both Lou and I felt very violated. I never told Wally, and there never were any results of any police investigation.

I very much wanted a pet. Lou's allergies were a consideration. We finally at Christmas time did get two guinea pigs, and then another. They were very lovable. Lou was able to tolerate them well and loved them. The first two were named Poinsettia and Mistletoe. I enjoyed showing Raeanne, Lou's granddaughter (then about three), how to hold it on a towel on her lap and stroke it gently. When one and later another died, Lou took it very hard.

• • •

Changes for Paula and Lynn: Paula, in her second year at Oberlin College, took the spring semester off to do a real-life study of intentional communities.

She visited and stayed a while at several, for example, Walden I, The Farm, and a women's shelter in Washington, D.C. Lynn was just finishing high school and ready to start at college. In the fall, I made a major trip with both girls. I drove Lynn to Mount Holyoke, and then Paula to Kennedy Airport. Paula drove part of the way, and on our way through Connecticut, we ran into what was left of a hurricane coming from the south, with tremendous winds and rain. Paula drove successfully during part of it but we were forced to stop at a rest center. We got to Kennedy on time, though, and Paula went with other students to a student exchange program for a semester in Denmark.

I received good letters from Paula about every six weeks. At the end of the semester, she decided to fly to Israel, then hitchhike back across Europe to the Netherlands, thus taking off a full year and a half from college. She used her savings and didn't try to work. She had many good and bad experiences and in March or April, I failed to get a letter. I was in Brockport on the day I started really worrying, and I called the U.S. State Department. They promised to be helpful, for which I was grateful. The next day I did get a letter and called them back. She didn't write of all her experiences, especially the bad ones. I learned of some of them years later.

In August 1980, Lynn and I flew to Germany to meet Paula and also Lou, who had been traveling in South Africa. The worst incident was being in a foreign airport trying to find Paula. Lynn and I got separated with a huge glass between us. I tried paging Paula. When I finally found her and met up with Lynn, Paula was in a section not getting the page. To be all together was a huge relief after a scary hour or so.

We did some sight-seeing and visited some friends Paula made in Germany and met Lou at another airport. Lou and I bought two lovely little wine glasses at an antique place. Then the four of us drove the Autobahn at eighty mph across Germany to the Netherlands. We went through Anne Frank's house in Amsterdam, which I found very moving. Then we flew back to the USA. Back home, from carelessness, I broke one of those beautiful wine glasses. I felt terrible.

Lynn took off a year, 1981-82, between her second and third years of college "to find herself" much as Paula had done. She found an apartment in Boston, found other renters, and ran into many household problems. These included a heater that went on the fritz, cockroaches, escaping gas, and deserting roommates. She got a job with a not-for-profit named "Nine-to-Five," which involved walking house-to-house for solicitations. It was certainly a year of growth and experience. She also took Dutch lessons while in Boston in preparation for the next year's student exchange.

A major set of revelations came to me during the girls' college careers. Each of them let me know about at the time of their graduations that each is a lesbian. I had suspected so for Paula, but not Lynn. This I learned to

Lynn, Jared, Paula — Paula's graduation

Lynn, Sid, Al, Paula

adjust to and come to terms with over the next several years. My main concern, which caused me deep distress, was my wish for grandchildren.

In June 1982, a year and a half after Wally and I separated, but just as the separation became official, Paula graduated magna cum laude from Oberlin after majoring in sociology/anthropology. It was the last time all four of us (Wally, both daughters, and me) were together and had a photo taken. Paula went almost immediately to start graduate school at the University of Michigan at Ann Arbor, aiming for a doctorate in sociology. Paula was in space more distant from home than Lynn during her dissertation years, but I felt a close bond. She had two or three different partners at University of Michigan. Then in 1983 she met Dr. Lorna Rodriguez, a gynecological surgeon, native of Puerto Rico, doing a post-doc fellowship. They soon decided they would be partners for life. I liked Lorna a lot as soon as I met her. Paula was being very activist in areas having to do with employment of gay people and even went to the Michigan State Legislature to testify on behalf of her fellow employees in a restaurant where she was a waitress, where some had been fired because of their sexual orientation.

Lynn's junior year at college, second semester, she spent in the Netherlands under Inter-future, a very interesting students' abroad program. Lynn did research, by interviews (in Dutch; that's why she took Dutch lessons while in Boston) with women about birth control. Then as part of the same program, she spent the summer in Jamaica interviewing for the same research question. She found conditions, attitudes, and resources in the two countries to be vastly different. Over the next several years, she maintained connections with Inter-future, got to know the staff well, and sat on their Board of Directors, attending meetings. One of the staff died of AIDS, and Lynn grieved.

In June of 1984, Lynn graduated magna cum Laude from Mount Holyoke, having double -majored in biology and Women's Studies. Wally had recently remarried (not having invited his daughters). Wally and his wife, Laurel, came together to Lynn's graduation. Paula, Lou, and I went together. In organizing Lynn's belongings to take home, Wally and I had to work together. Laurel stayed in their car, so I met her only momentarily. I had hoped to get acquainted with her. I have a photo of a very proud Lynn receiving her diploma.

Lynn came to Lou's and my home, had some wisdom teeth pulled, and convalesced for a few weeks. Then she got a job as a technician in the Pediatric Hematology-Oncology lab at Strong, moved to an apartment, and began trying to decide whether to go to graduate school. In 1986 Lynn decided to go ahead and get her doctorate in microbiology at the University of Rochester.

After Paula finished her course work in 1986 and was starting her dissertation, Lorna took a fellowship at Albert Einstein Medical Center in New

York City. They moved in 1986 to Larchmont, a town in Westchester County near Lorna's hospital. Paula was in constant contact with her advisor by computer. Her thesis was a questionnaire study of bisexuality, which became her major field. She and Lorna had a lovely little black part poodle that Paula had rescued from an abusive situation in Ann Arbor, named Artie (for Artemis). They lived in a rented place for a while, then bought a house.

During this period, Paula got another dog to train to be a "companion" dog. She was a beautiful black Lab, six weeks old, named Inca. Paula's job was to socialize her and get her used to many environments. At eighteen months, she would return her to the organization for more formal training. Inca wore a yellow jacket identifying her as a companion dog. She grew and learned very well. She and Artie got along after Artie, being smaller, had some initial apprehension. Inca was well loved. When she was returned ready to be trained, the trainers told Paula she was unusually well prepared, but unfortunately had hip problems shown by x-ray. Many Labradors do have that. She would not be able to do companion work for long, so she was returned to Paula, who wanted her with family at least. Lynn took her in 1988 and cared for her in LeRoy, New York, where she then lived with Kathy, her current partner.

• • •

More Career Advances: In the next time period I started to help at Strong in the supervision and training of Family Practice residents, doing their psychiatry rotations. Dr. Jan Feigelson had been doing this for a while, and we continued it together. She and I became close friends. I later continued as Clinical Assistant Professor in Psychiatry to carry out other supervisory endeavors.

One of my other activities was giving monthly lectures for the therapy staff of Catholic Family Services, starting after I had been supervising one of them in therapy. At my private office I supervised a few other young therapists. I was not great at supervising, but some of my lectures were good. I still had some stage fright, but compared with how I was in high school, I did vastly better!

I did psychiatric consults at Brockport Memorial, Park Ridge, and Genesee Hospitals, and much later at Rochester General and Highland.

In Brockport at Western Monroe, I was seeing a number of developmentally disabled patients. They all lived in a group home. As I worked more in Greece, more such people from other group homes came to see me. I had contacts with Dr. Nancy Cain at Strong. She was in charge of the program (therapy, medicines, consults) for these people at Strong. She was able to get me a year's fellowship from the state to work with her. I learned a lot about this population and went on to see more and more developmentally disabled people both at Western Monroe and in my private practice. I made a few house calls to group homes, and developed an interest in autism.

A friend, Jean Lake, whose husband had served as Wally's best man at our wedding, had a very strong interest in autistic young adults. When I was at RPC in Unit C, I got to know a young autistic man. He turned out to be Calvin, the three-year-old I had examined at the Strong Therapeutic Nursery back many years before! Jean had a special interest in him too. I supervised her work with him. Starting with him she made a thorough study of autism, gave lectures all over the world, and established the Autistic Habilitation Center, which for a number of years held one to two-week summer camps for half a dozen or so young adults with autism. They came from various hospitals and group homes around the state. Using techniques Jean developed, almost all the campers progressed in speech and/or behavior, even in the one or two weeks. I sat for those years on her Board of Directors.

Beth's husband developed a malignant bone tumor in his arm. Beth underwent a year of extreme stress. Her boss was Timothy Madden, of the Park Ridge administration. He had different ideas than she did about Western Monroe's growth. Hers were very idealistic, including education of the therapists and their growth as therapists, and we had team meetings for case discussions. Madden said they cost too much. Finally, after Beth's husband died, Madden talked to each of the other three in our administration (the Controller, Marcia Ilardo; Program Manager, Gordon Barnhart; and me) saying that he was planning to let Beth go.

The day she was told to leave, I was in Brockport and didn't see her. I wish I had gone to her to support her. I didn't realize until much later that I was really important to her and that that would have been helpful to her.

For a time then, three of us ran the operation. I think we did okay, maintaining the high level of service the therapists had developed.

• • •

A New Era: Beth asked me to meet her for dinner at the Lamplighter Restaurant. She presented me with an offer I couldn't very well refuse. She and Joyce DuBrin (my therapist), and another woman, Trudy Baran, a psychologist, were planning to set up a practice together. They wanted me to join them as medical director and supervisor! It did take me a long time to think about it because of ramifications, the most important of which was that it was professionally improper for me to play two different roles with Joyce (i.e. therapist-patient and working partner). This would in the future turn into a big problem.

I finally did accept with excitement. I would transfer my private practice to theirs, with Dick Kepner. An old building was to be gutted and lovely offices made. The four of us met for breakfast weekly, planning and getting acquainted. Trudy became another good friend.

Beth, Joyce, and Trudy (and Joyce's husband, Bob) advocated and used certain therapy techniques that expanded on the usual. They wrote a book about it. They used hugs and holding, especially down on the mat. They encouraged the full expression of feelings, like crying or screaming in anger or pounding into a pillow. I gradually began to use the same techniques with certain patients, and when I led groups, because they were effective. I did groups during the annual week-long marathons, held at a nearby college. At one of these, I discovered from my "Psychiatric News" that my friend Nancy R. had died. This I actively grieved about. The next group session that day, Joyce allowed me to participate as her patient, so I could really express my grief. Sad as it was, real grief was a good experience.

The new practice opened in the fall of 1983 with a great reception. We named it Park Alexander Therapy Services (at the intersection of those two streets). Dick Kepner and Dr. Susan Hanson, a psychiatrist friend of Beth, shared office space with us. Lou made a very original "No Smoking" sign for the lobby which I later kept.

Wally came to the reception, but asked that Lou not come at the same time. He blamed her for our break-up. The divorce papers came to me in December 1983, via a marshal who evidently thought I was going to refuse them. He came to Western Monroe and asked for me to come out front. When I insisted I be told who he was, he left. Twice. The next day he was waiting for me in the parking lot and served me very abruptly. I felt demeaned. The papers could have been mailed to me, according to my lawyer.

Meanwhile, a search committee was established at Park Ridge to find a new Western Monroe Executive Director under Madden. There were two major candidates, both being doctors in the Psychiatric Department at Strong. I interviewed both. One I knew well—Alex—he had been my psychotherapy tutor after Syracuse. He was idealistic, with wonderful expectations building on what Beth had achieved. The other candidate I knew a little. He was much more the type that would kow-tow to Madden. In a major Board meeting, I said the second would be more moldable than the first. I felt I was saving Alex from a life of frustration and discouragement but I never had the opportunity to let him know that. The second one, Dr. Tom Gift, was chosen, and the bloom gradually disappeared. Western Monroe slowly became a business instead of an oasis for people.

• • •

Vacation Trips: In the eighties, and early nineties, Lou and I took some memorable summer vacation trips. One summer my cousin Bill invited me to go with him to the Grand Canyon. I asked if Lou could go with us, and he agreed. Lou and I flew to Louisville, met him there, and rented a car—a big one because he's so tall. It was a good trip, with one exception. Lou and I had signed up for one of the mule trips down into the canyon. We thought we had prepared for this by taking some horseback rides in Rochester to accustom our muscles to it. We found out that in riding a mule down a steep path and then riding up the path, we had to use two entirely new and different sets of muscles. I felt tortured and in pain a short while after starting. One mule, at the rear end, got spooked and galloped along the very edge of the narrow path, stopping only when he got to the head of the line. That was scary! It also was unnerving as we approached a sharp turn to look over the mule's head and see nothing but space, no terra firma in sight, and moving closer and closer until we actually rounded the bend. It's interesting to remember and record that trip, but it wasn't fun. Bill was wise to not do it.

We also saw Zion (all the roads were red), Bryce (where the mountains are brilliant red; Lou painted it at home, and I have the painting), and Arches National Parks.

One trip was to the beautiful Canadian Rockies. Lou and I took an overnight train from Toronto to Calgary and rented a car. We drove north to Banff. Glorious scenery. We saw Lake Louise, with glaciers in the distance. We saw Athabasca Falls, which later Lou painted for me—it's my favorite painting. It hung in my private office until I retired. After Athabasca, we drove through more mountains to Vancouver, visited Vancouver Island, and flew home.

Another trip was to Alaska. We flew into Fairbanks first and took a train south to Anchorage. On that part of the trip the train stopped at Denali State Park, where we took a bus ride in. We saw a wolf, but no other wildlife. In Anchorage, we boarded a cruise ship to go through the inner waterways. We got real close to a calving glacier, a mysteriously terrifying sight. "Calving" is like the birth—breaking off—of a large piece of glacier to become an iceberg. We flew home again from Vancouver.

In the late eighties Lou and I took a very memorable two-week trip to Hawaii. The first week was sponsored by the Nature Conservancy and we knew it would involve endurance hiking. So we prepared for it for several weeks on Lou's exercycle. But the week before we left we were sick with colds, without energy to cycle much. So we lost much of that preparation. We were not adequately ready for the endurance needed.

We flew to Maui and met our group of about eight people (including us) and leader in a hotel. The leader, a woman, was a naturalist, very well-informed about the field and about Hawaii, with a very supportive persona. The rest of the group was couples, mostly retired but healthy, with good insights and knowledge, all eager to learn a lot. Our first day was a trip to a lava field. There are two kinds of cold lava, pillow and ah-ah. The former is smooth with rounded edges and grooves. The latter is a jammed full field of helter-skelter, sharp-edged, and pointed rocks scattered in large groups. I chose not to walk on it, but adventurous Lou did. She tripped and fell down onto sharp edges and points and broke three ribs. So our trip was interrupted by long-distance driving by our leader to take Lou to the only hospital on the island for confirmatory x-rays and the statement that there's nothing to do for broken ribs.

She endured, although she was in great pain. For one hike, she came up the mountain by helicopter, meeting the rest of us at the top. We hiked up and through tropical forest, wet and hot. We saw muddy places with no plants where feral pigs had wallowed and made mud holes. The Nature Conservancy is a world-wide organization, with regional chapters, which buys up land that is ecologically endangered and valuable, and then arranges to maintain it in its pristine state. It works to repair some of the damage already done, such as getting rid of non-native species, like the feral pigs, if possible.

Hawaii has had bad experiences with introduced, non-native plants and animals. The native birds are almost extinct. We hoped to see some on one of the hikes but did not. The hotels have birds chirping in their gardens, but they are all recordings. I have friends, however, who did find many birds in Hawaii, many of which were probably not native.

We saw some features of each of the islands except the Big Island the first week. One trip was to Molokai, the island where the leper colony is. There are still some people living there for whom it has been home for many years, but no new people, as there is now good treatment for leprosy.

After the first week was over, we said goodbyes to our group and especially the wonderful leader. Lou and I were ready to sit down, rest, and put our feet up. We found a lodge on the Big Island close to a beautiful, inactive, volcanic crater. Lou painted it after being back home. My ankles swelled to enormous size. We did make a few short excursions, one to the foot of the constantly active volcano of Mauna Loa, where hot red lava was continually flowing into the sea. What a fabulous sight that was! We also saw native species of plants in bloom. We took a helicopter flight over the peaks of Kawai, peaks made by erosion into many sharp ridges. The scenery everywhere is highly variable, but at all places spectacular.

We flew home, with Lou's now-healing ribs and my now-swelling ankles, which lasted a week or more at home. But in spite of these leftovers, we had had a fabulous trip.

On other shorter trips, Lou accompanied me to the annual summer Cape Cod Psychiatric Symposia. We stayed at first in motels, then bought a small trailer camper and camped there. The first time we took the camper, the hitch broke at the eastern end of the highway in Massachusetts. Luckily we also had put on a chain, but the camper weaved itself across much of the road. Fortunately there was little traffic. We had to get it towed quite a distance to a repair place and had to stay overnight at a motel, missing one day of the conference. We also did other weekend camping trips, mostly nearer to home.

We went to Sanibel Island in Florida twice and saw the wonderful birds; to Myrtle Beach; and Chincoteague where the wild horses live, in the Barrier Islands.

• • •

Fortieth High School Anniversary and Reunion: In 1985, my high school planned a Great Reunion for all the classes. It was a huge project. Activities abounded. Some classes, like ours, were special, ours being fortieth. Our class had never had a reunion.

They planned it a year ahead and ex-students learned about it early on. I must lose twenty pounds in preparation. Weight Loss Clinic prescribed for me one of the more drastic diets. The counselors wore white and dealt with all kinds of charts. I was started on a 500-calorie diet. Lou, who cooked for us because she enjoyed it, saw that we adhered to it. She had twenty pounds as her goal too. After two days I was almost a basket case. Then we remembered to add the special salt, and I came back to myself. Lou and I each did lose twenty pounds in about three months.

For the Reunion weekend, we planned a special long weekend trip. Lou, who was a talented artist, wanted to paint nature. We had the camper trailer, which opens up into a tent. We found the right woodsy place in southwest New York. We opened up the tent and set up Lou's painting materials, and then I drove on to Chatham, leaving her there without a car. For her, it was a lousy weekend. After I left, it rained; Lou found we had forgotten her antidepressant; and the tent collapsed. And she didn't have a car or telephone. Or a TV.

I had a fantastically wonderful time. The only bad spots were finding that two members and one husband had died. The first was Bill M., who had been president of the senior class and had become a hospital manager, then died of a brain tumor. The second was Ricky D., who had lived near me. He had also had a surprisingly illustrious career (in school he had been a wise guy whose grades did not match his potential), then died early of some lingering GI disease. I really missed connecting with those two. My childhood girlfriend, Gert, had married and then lost her husband in a terrible traffic accident. After she told me this, she changed the subject. Gloria was also present; that was a joyful reunion. I was friendly and talkative, unlike my usual self, and felt remembered and liked by many.

We had a gala dinner under a tent. Gert sat next to me. I did not get to talk to Bailey because he did not come, but I connected with several others. One, Ruth P., I recognized immediately because of her smile with wrinkled eyes. I found out that two of the mainstreamed special ed girls now lived in group homes. Another friend, Shirley D., with whom I've kept up regularly, was there. Another, Joan B., had had a fascinating life, with some aspects similar to my own, like lesbian daughters. She was an ordained minister (and preached Sunday morning of the reunion). She and her husband had run an inner-city church, with shelter and food for the homeless, and all kinds of outreach, until she had two heart attacks and got herself divorced to become a university dean. Her Sunday sermon was about the reunion and that more was going on than just remaking old ties.

I returned to Lou with her news of the awful weekend. I was shocked. We went into town to fill her prescription and at my suggestion, she took a slightly larger dose to try to make up some of what she had missed. Then she got sick to her stomach. She felt so miserable that I finished taking down the tent and we went home a day early. I felt terribly guilty that I'd had a wonderful weekend and she such a lousy one.

$$\bullet \quad \bullet \quad \bullet$$

New Parts of Life: Lou had a friend who was just learning to use a new Mac Performa computer. Lou was so intrigued and enthusiastic about it that she convinced me we should get one, and we did! We had a great time setting it up and learning it. We bought *Macs for Dummies* and learned a lot. Lou used the computer a lot for graphics and art inventory. I used it for databases on my patients. We both used it for correspondence and documents and exploring the Internet. I found a very fine Mac consultant on whom I called many times for trouble-shooting and lessons, named Steve Gem. I bought a digital piano and software called "Encore" sold me by a friend (Kate Schroeder's husband Terrence) to use in composing music. It never worked really as I wanted it to and as it was supposed to.

I was able to visit Paula and Lorna in Larchmont a few times. One time Lorna asked me about my misgivings about grandchildren, and we had a very emotional and satisfying discussion. Another time, Connie D, the therapist who was also a close friend and a member of our Women's Issues group (see below), went with me to Larchmont for a weekend. The purpose was to visit my mother's grave in Brooklyn and work on my feelings of hostility toward her. Two things happened that weekend: Connie and I had a highly fruitful discussion at the grave about my relationship with my mother (it was then that we figured out the importance of my reaction to her wanting to massage my feet); and, driving the car from Larchmont to Brooklyn, Connie observed that I drove with quick decisions and high confidence. She pointed out that that was unlike my administrative style, and it was no doubt due to the fact that my father had taught me to drive, not my mother. My mother really taught me to be passive. Connie made good friends with both girls.

I made another trip to my mother's grave, this time with just my dad. We had the most intimate conversation I've ever had with him. We talked a lot about Mom and their relationship. It was then that I learned that she knew more about sex than he did when they married and about his grief when her father died.

In the late eighties, Lou and I joined in the March on Washington to support women's rights to choose abortions. Joyce DuBrin and Beth Struever both went. We met the bus in a large parking lot down town at midnight. The bus was full. We traveled through the night, trying to sleep. We arrived just after dawn, in a line of buses from all over, slowly getting into another very large parking lot. As we approached it, I looked out the window and was able to see a line of buses in front of us and a very long line curving behind us. There were hundreds of buses! What a spectacle! It was inspiring!

We took the subway to the gathering place at the Washington Monument. I had never been in a crowd that large in close contact before. There were thousands of women, and I was seized by a wish to see how far I was from an edge of the crowd, but couldn't do so. It was an odd and somewhat frightening sensation. Finally we started moving up the Mall. Lou and I went by sidewalk. I could not have kept up with the main crowd. Finally we got to the Capitol Building. Nearby was a "graveyard" with many crosses and Stars of David, spread out there by anti-abortionists as if they were graves for aborted fetuses. We listened to some speeches but couldn't hear well. I think we got lunch from a vendor.

Toward the end of the day we made our way back to the bus, and after collecting all on board, started driving back to Rochester. The driver had not been able to sleep during the day, so was sleepy and driving slowly. A couple of women at the front of the bus kept up a conversation with him to keep him awake. Again, we didn't sleep much. It was a scary ride, and we were glad to get back to Rochester. It was a very memorable trip!

Toward the end of my employment at Western Monroe, I arranged for the senior therapists to have a weekly supervision with Dr. Otto Thaler, a top supervisor at Strong's Psychiatric Department. In my externship there many years before, he was the favored supervisor and did group supervision among the house staff, including myself, and also advised me in my treatment of one of my out-patients. In our W.M. group, each therapist, including me, chose one of their patients to tape an interview to bring to the meeting, one interview a week. This was well-received by the therapists, and I was pleased that I could wangle the money for it from the budget. I'm not sure now how I did that! It was the accomplishment I've been most proud of at Western Monroe, getting the money in spite of Madden, for a truly growth experience for the therapists. Otto brought his wife Lisl, a psychiatric social worker, to the meetings. I think the therapists gained a lot from that series.

Several years later, Otto developed a cancer, I think pancreatic. He had several treatments, but finally decided he'd had enough. Right after his last treatment, while he was in relative remission, the Department gave him a great reception and dinner at the top of the Strathallan Hotel. When I spoke to him, I thought I'd better give him my name. He replied, "Yes, of course I know you, Mildred." That was reward enough. He died a few months later.

At Western Monroe, one of my duties was to do a medication group facilitated by a therapist. My role was to take each woman (about twelve women made up the group) aside, talk with her briefly, and write her prescriptions. At the last meeting (see below), this group of patients gave me a lovely revolving music box!

My lack of proactive administrative skills became more and more observable, as I was more interested in the growth of staff and patients, and Madden and the new Director were more interested in the bottom line. I knew I lacked administrative skills. I was supposed to be doing something about making a plan for Quality Assurance. I talked a lot with Beth Struever about my misgivings and disappointments. Finally in 1986 I resigned with a quite provocative letter about my disillusionments re: Western Monroe, which I delivered to the Chairman of the Board (at Strong) and to Madden and to the new Director, the afternoon before the Board meeting. At the meeting the Director said he'd try to talk me out of it. But he met with me the next day, after he had obviously conferred with Madden after the Board meeting and instead of talking about my staying, demoted me, saying I would have clinical duties only for my two remaining weeks. I asked if I could finish a certain project I had been working on. He said that couldn't harm anything, so I could. Clearly Madden was afraid I would do something to sabotage the Center.

The staff of therapists and clerical workers gave me a wonderful dinner. Lou was invited. Connie emceed. What transpired was a series of people telling specific anecdotes about me, many of them being things I had done for them! They gave me beautiful gifts. The administrative staff didn't give me a dinner—it seemed inappropriate—but one of them took me to lunch and presented me with a plaque.

Later that year Connie, whom I had seen regularly for lunch, called me with an invitation to join a group of ex-Western Monroe therapists (several resigned before and after I did, for similar reasons), all of whom I knew well. They held monthly meetings at rotating homes, to discuss topics of interest, case histories that needed some feedback, or personal problems. The others in the group were Martha Tollers, Caroll Revak, Mary Garber, and Beth Jelsma. Besides Connie, I had had lunches and breakfasts with Beth J. and Mary. The group was already tight-knit, but I fitted in effortlessly. The group became extremely bonded. I call it our women's issues group. Others call it a study group, or similar terms.

I continued my private practice at Park Alexander. For several months I participated in a drug study for a pharmaceutical company. The goal was to determine the best dose for Paxil, an antidepressant, which was to reach the market shortly. It was laborious, with the need for lots of paperwork and preciseness in drug dosing. I ended up including only two people that fit the criteria, one of whom had to have an emergency cholecystectomy (gall bladder) in the middle, so the drug had to be discontinued, but he'd already responded well to it. I just hope my results were useful!

Changing Continued

Soon after leaving Western Monroe in 1986, I learned of an open position for a psychiatrist at Wilson Health Center, which was sort of associated with Rochester General Hospital. It provided general treatment for a large population, and included a Psychiatric Department. I was readily hired and got to know another group of wonderful therapists. We met regularly for departmental discussions and occasionally for case discussions.

My work at Park Alexander Therapy Services went well. At some point, Dick Kepner decided to move to California where his parents now lived. I've continued a Christmas card friendship with him. At Park Alexander, we had a short series of secretaries. The best was Ruth Ann Downs, who stayed with PATS and then later worked with each of us individually.

After the PATS' six-year lease was up, we decided there were enough faults with the building to not renew it. After some looking and conferencing, we decided on Beth's suggestion that she renovate her house to include offices. She did this in 1988, and we moved. It was a comfortable arrangement. I had a downstairs office under the stairs, but had to go up and down to talk with the secretary and for our conferences. It was beginning to get harder for me to climb stairs, because of weight gain and feelings of weakness and stiffness in my legs.

In our previous office building, we had shared space with another psychiatrist, Dr. Sue Hanson. She learned that my sixtieth birthday was coming up (February 14, 1988). She very generously planned a birthday party at her house, to which Joyce, Beth, and Trudy were invited. I arrived last and greeted my colleagues; then suddenly others appeared—Lou and Connie D., from the next room. It was a lovely surprise. We had a very good dinner and good dinner conversation.

About then I began to realize I had difficulty hearing, especially with a noisy or static background. I had several hearing tests over the years, which were always normal, and finally realized I've had a mild tinnitus for probably most of my life. It interfered with hearing. At one point, I bought a "listening device" I could set on the table and with earphones hear individuals somewhat better, but not much. I used it only a few times.

I discovered I had cataracts. I had them removed and artificial implants placed. These were done a year apart at an ambulatory medical center. Lou accompanied me on both these occasions. Immediately after each surgery I was amazed at the improvement in vision, especially the greater brightness of colors. I deeply regretted that my mother's had not done well, although of course her surgery didn't use the modern techniques that mine did.

Trudy Baran had dropped out of Park Alexander to form her own practice about 1988. She still came to conferences. She had had a mastectomy and chemotherapy several years before. We knew she had recurrences of the cancer and was being given "palliative radiology." In June of 1996 or 1997, she announced to Beth S. and me that she had been told she had about six months to live and fought back tears. Beth held her for a time. In a few weeks she was admitted to the hospice at St. Mary's Hospital. I visited several times and did better at such conversations than I had done previously. She really came to terms with death and died in September (only three months instead of six) and appeared to die comfortably. I went to her memorial service at Temple B'rith Kodesh, and I did grieve.

• • •

Major Shifts in My Offices: In 1990 I decided to change my working arrangements with Park Alexander and to move to another group of psychologists I knew who were building a new office building on Monroe Avenue in Brighton. I wanted to get out of the double role with Joyce, because it was harder to be a director. I thought the new arrangement would be somewhat more prestigious in location and credentials (all were psychologists and one other was a psychiatrist) and one of them, Beth Jelsma, was a very close friend. I expected and assumed therapy would continue with Joyce.

In March I announced this to Beth S. and Joyce. For some reason, I didn't fully anticipate the degree of Beth's and Joyce's angry and sad reactions to my decision. Joyce required me to terminate from therapy, which I had not expected, both individual and group, over a period of a few months. She blamed me for 'terminating" even though, way back while I was considering joining her, Beth, and Trudy, she had specifically answered my question about such a situation, saying such a decision on my part would not affect my therapy. It was of course resulting from our improper decision on roles at that previous time.

There was a massive strain on our relationships at PATS, especially between me and Joyce. I tried my best to hide my feelings, but they both saw through that. Beth tried various ways to mollify me and Joyce's anger.

In June 1990, Lou and I went on a planned trip to Cape Cod, as we had done other years. Starting with Joyce's termination announcement to me, I had cried continuously in the car and at home. On the trip I cried all the way, and Lou wouldn't let me drive. It suddenly occurred to me that not only was it (June 16) Lynn's birthday, it was also the anniversary of my mother's death. I called Frances from a pay phone to confirm that. Later I also called Dad. On our return I kept the first appointment with Dr. Ray Babineau, whom I had known slightly. He helped me through this awful period. I was then in weekly therapy with him until my move to New Jersey, and I now see him periodically on my visits back to Rochester.

In July 1990, Lou and I took a cruise ship from Los Angeles with the sole purpose of seeing the total solar eclipse from the best place in the world, just off the tip of Baja California. Everyone on the ship came for the same reason. We had lectures, etc. The expensive shops and bars on the boat didn't get much business on that trip. The eclipse was magnificent. We indeed had the best spot in the world. Another ship farther out in the Pacific was partly clouded over. This trip occurred during my grief about Joyce, but I was able to enjoy its specialness.

Now that I was no longer in the therapy group, I was able to rejoin the church choir, which I did in September 1990. It provided much support. It rehearsed on the therapy group's previous evening time.

Beth arranged an interview with a professional mediator in December 1990 to try to help us work together more peacefully. At that meeting I announced that I would move to another office on Alexander St. in January 1991, even though the first new office wasn't ready yet.

In January 1991, I moved my office to a therapists' group in the Medical Arts Building on Alexander Street near where the PATS' first office had been. This group was very welcoming. I explained the situation to them, that I would be there temporarily until the other new office became ready. I was able to transfer my patients easily, on minimal explanation. I was finally able to move, with Beth J. and the others, to Monroe Avenue, in July 1992, again transferring patients. I lost one patient because of a misunderstanding about scheduling.

After I had left, the therapy group had been broken up by Joyce and the members decided to meet weekly, leaderless but including me, at the Medical Arts Building for a while.

On March 1, 1991, Lou and I woke very early because of the storm noise outside. It was still dark, but outside it was very bright because of the ice. We looked out the back window over the meadow and woods and saw ice coating everything, and trees breaking and falling down. Rochester declared an emergency, as many streets were not passable. Many power lines were down. We were without power for a couple of days, but many were without it for a week. I had an appointment scheduled with Ray that day, and I wanted very much to keep it, even knowing non-emergency driving was forbidden. I called Ray, and said if he could make it, I could too. He agreed and we did meet, in an empty building.

During the two years of my grief, I received great support from many of my friends, including Lou and those in the WI group. It came up only once in the meetings though. Connie told a beautiful allegorical story to help me with it. I also ate handfuls of nuts, which I love, and gained ten more pounds of weight over the two years.

I was able to begin crying less eighteen months after the termination process started, and six months later I felt recovered.

In 1992, I retired from the Wilson Health Center after six years there. They gave me a dinner and a plaque.

· · ·

Family Changes: Al and Sid, Wally's parents, were getting into their nineties. Sid suffered from severe osteoporosis, breaking bones often, and finding her chest increasingly crushed, making breathing a serious problem. Her mother and sister also had it. I visited her in the Hamot Hospital (in Erie) twice, once with Lou, Paula, and Lorna. Both times Al was with her. He was there constantly. Sid could barely speak and couldn't move. Nurses turned her regularly. Lorna tried to feed her some jello, but she choked on just a little. Lorna said something enthusiastically, teasing her about getting the right food, and Sid exclaimed, "You do that!" a phrase she often used. She sounded just like her old self, though much weaker. That may have been her last words, because generally she wasn't talking at all, Al said. She died in the hospital a few days later, in 1992.

Lynn at that time had broken her ankle in a motorcycle accident and was on crutches. I took her and Paula to Sid's memorial service in a funeral chapel in Erie. Wally, his wife, and Iola, Wally's twelve-year-younger sister, were there. Al and Sid had not been churchgoers and had no affiliation. Al engaged a young woman Unitarian minister and told her about Sid. The service was simple and lovely. Al grieved mightily for the rest of his life. He died a few years later in an assisted living place.

· · ·

Professional Activities: Throughout my career, I had been consulting with two organizations: Compeer, a non-profit which matched patients, usually outpatients, with a volunteer "friend;" and the "Work and Social Adjustment Program," which helped discharged patients prepare themselves to go to work, and try in monitored jobs to adjust. Both of these I had started working with back at RPC, starting with my partnership with the chaplain. While

I was at Western Monroe, Compeer asked me to represent them on the Board of the IMH, described above when I thought about joining Western Monroe. This met monthly, but was a five-year pilot project with temporary state funding, after which it went unfunded. There were attempts to continue, but it slowly fell apart. With the WSAP, I had met monthly for conferences on pertinent topics, one of which I did was the structure of sleep. (I also did the one on sleep for RPC's Unit C staff.) I retired officially from them in 1997. They took me to dinner and gave me a camera.

My private practice was growing substantially and more rapidly after the move to Monroe Avenue in July 1992. I was getting many referrals from many therapists whose patients appeared to need medication. Most of the therapists were trained by me one way or another and were almost always right about the need for medication. I was working essentially full-time at my private office. I took on the supervision of two psychiatric nurse practitioners who obtained the necessary credentials to prescribe meds but required continuing supervision. One of them, Kate Schroeder, I knew very well, as she had worked at Western Monroe. The other I hadn't known until I took this on. It was an interesting arrangement. I saw them monthly, with telephone calls in between.

●　　●　　●

More Milestones for Paula and Lynn: After Paula finished her dissertation and got her degree in 1989, she took a job as Assistant Professor of Sociology at Hamilton College in Clinton, New York, which meant she had to commute by the week from Larchmont, where they had moved to in 1986.

When Lorna, Paula's partner, finished her fellowship at Einstein, she decided to do a doctorate in gynecologic HIV at the University of Rochester, and they moved to Rochester in 1991. Paula resigned her Hamilton job just as she got tenure. She took a similar job as Assistant Professor at the State University at Geneseo and commuted from Rochester. It was very good for me to have them living so near me. Lorna's parents moved from Puerto Rico to Rochester soon after, and I began to become acquainted with them.

Her father, Paco, knew little English and doesn't converse with me very much. Her mother, Raquel, does much better with English and loves to talk to me. We bonded quite well, even though at times I have trouble understanding her. When they and Lorna are present together, they speak Spanish. Although both Paula and I had taken Spanish in high school, we couldn't converse in it. I frequently felt left out of family gatherings because of this, but got used to it.

Lynn had a series of female partners, all of whom I liked. I frequently met her for breakfast, and I felt close to her. She did her dissertation on an aspect of *Pseudomonas aeroginosa* (a ubiquitous and important bacterium). She finished her dissertation in 1993, but her defense was two weeks too late for her to get her diploma in 1993, so she received it by mail in 1994. She then started a post-doc in the biochemistry department. Meanwhile Lynn had left Inca with Kathy, her recent partner, in 1992. My friend Beth Jelsma's daughter Flynn was wanting a Lab, so it was arranged she would take Inca. Inca lived happily, in a loving family, with excellent behavior, for the rest of her life, with Flynn.

Paula and Lorna had decided they would have children, to my great delight, and applied to an agency in Philadelphia for adoption. Paula, after several attempts, got pregnant by artificial insemination. This was in 1995. Lou and I gave her and Lorna a baby shower at our house in late fall, attended by friends of mine and theirs. Lou made a huge banner by computer, welcoming the "Mommies" and hung it over the fireplace. Those who hadn't known Lorna were delighted by her antics, wit, and charm. (Well, we all were!)

In December, when Paula was five months pregnant, they were called that an adoptable baby was available in Philadelphia. I went with them, and we stayed at Frances' house. I went with them to the agency attorney's home and met Mykelti Antonio Rodriguez Rust, one day old, on December 22, 1995. Mykelti was a lovely black baby whose hair was absolutely straight. It kinked up after several months. Fran said, "He's a very lucky baby." Paula and Lorna had to stay in Philadelphia a few days for paperwork reasons and before leaving were stymied by a blizzard, in which nobody could drive. I had already flown back to Rochester for my work, but they came back three weeks later.

They hired a nanny, Wilma, a Puerto Rican. She was very good. Sometimes her husband, Dave, who was disabled because of a back problem, came with her. As the children grew, they became very fond of her.

A few months later, Paula observed that Artie, the dog, was getting defiant and had growled and bared his teeth at her. No doubt this had to do with jealousy of Mykelti's presence. Paula was understandably alarmed, and decided she had to give him up. An attempt was made by their vet first to place him with another family. Artie couldn't adjust, however, and didn't behave well. Paula asked the vet to take him back and euthanize him without telling her when. I was very unhappy about this turn of events. Artie had been a lovable, obedient pet for many years.

Paula's pregnancy proceeded with minor complications, and she went into labor April 18, 1996. Lorna and I and several of Paula's friends took her to the hospital (Strong). Lorna's mother stayed with Mykelti. Paula's experience was very different from my experiences! She had a mini-suite with many comforts. Lorna's mother brought four new dresses she had made, for photos of the four (including Mykelti) after the delivery. Paula had support from all present throughout her labor. When she was ready to push, the obstetrician asked her to slow down, but instead the baby actually came precipitously, and Paula suffered quite a tear. The doctor abruptly left and sent in a resident to sew her up.

Later, the head nurse, a male, told the group that he was favorably impressed with the amount of support there for Paula. The baby girl's name would be Saraiah Raquel. While holding her in a chair, I dozed and she slipped down to the floor, which scared me when she hit the floor with a whomp and woke me. She was examined by a pediatrician who found a minor bruise but assured me she was okay. I watched her first bath, given very thoroughly and lovingly by a nurse.

Lorna finished her dissertation (on HIV) and graduated in June 1996. I attended as faculty, wearing the robe with green hood (for medicine), in the faculty procession. I felt very proud of Lorna and my family. Lorna then became Director of Gynecology-oncology at Strong.

Two or three summers I went with Paula and Lorna to the annual Michigan Women's Music Festival, with Lou and Lynn once, and Saraiah and Mykelti once. We camped and used hundreds of port-a-potties in a long line. There were thousands of women there. One time a deluge of sudden rain flooded out a concert in the middle, and in gathering my stuff I lost a beautiful large tote bag that had been a retirement gift to Lou from her school colleagues. It had her name on it in big block letters. I went back later, couldn't find it, and even posted notices in a newsletter. I felt terrible about losing it.

Lynn went to a microbiology conference in California in 1995 and met a man, Eric Garber, about her age, and also a microbiologist. She came home and told me, "I met someone." Eric had a university job in West Virginia. They traveled back and forth for several weeks. When her fellowship was up she moved to West Virginia to live with him. Her friends in Rochester gave her a royal send-off, and Eric came to help in the move. Society's attitudes had changed so much, and I too, that her living with him didn't faze me. I don't know her thoughts about her sexual orientation. Lynn got a job as research assistant professor at Marshall University in West Virginia and started looking for a permanent faculty job. Eric and Lynn obtained a beautiful mixed black dog named Diogenes. He is part Australian sheep dog.

Several months later she got a wonderful offer from North Dakota State University in the Department of Veterinarian and Microbiological Sciences, an offer "I can hardly bear to refuse," as she said to me. She did move to Fargo, and she and Eric resumed their long-distance relationship. During this time Eric and Lynn adopted another black dog, a mixed breed, also totally black but much smaller than Diogenes. They named her Nisse, after a Scandanavian gnome. Eric tried and tried to find a job in Fargo and finally got one in 1999 at the USDA and moved into the house Lynn had

Diogenes

Nisse

bought. At that time both were happy with their jobs, and from then on both dogs were part of the family.

· · ·

Lou's Illness: Backing up a bit, Lou had come once to Paula's hospital delivery room, but she wasn't feeling well and didn't stay. That previous Christmas, Lou had had a severe asthma attack in our basement, from something down there. She had to crawl up the stairs, but was relieved after being upstairs for a while. Both of us were overweight again, at approximately 140 pounds. We started dieting and both of us lost some weight. In January 1996, Lou was hospitalized twice at Brockport Memorial with pneumonia. I noticed after a while that she was continuing to lose weight to less than her goal. I began to feel alarmed. In addition she was feeling abdominal pain when eating. She went to her doctor who first gave her ulcer medicine; when that didn't work, her gall bladder was removed. The pain and weight loss continued, and in the course of three days over a weekend the three doctors in that practice gave her three different antibiotics. That was the last straw. They never did do a satisfactory work-up. I was furious.

I felt I had to immediately have her transferred to an internist at Genesee Hospital, Dr. Betty Rabinowitz, whom I knew and trusted. Lou's daughters, Glynne and Jessie, were also more and more concerned, and Glynne personally went to the old doctors' office to insist on getting Lou's records for the new doctor. A work-up was started, but no one thought of an abdominal angiogram. Home Health nurses came to the house and installed a feeding line in her neck, but that night she vomited bile and was very weak. She was hospitalized at Genesee Hospital and was receiving parenteral (by intravenous lines) feedings. I visited her every day after seeing my patients. Several doctors were consulted. Finally a vascular surgeon, Dr. Thomas Penn, did an angiogram of the abdomen and discovered she had a blocked artery to liver, stomach, and spleen, so that digestion could not work. In November surgery was performed and a stent placed at the blockage. She recovered enough to go back from ICU to her regular bed. On a Sunday, a friend of hers and I were there. We were encouraged that she was conversing some with us. After the friend had gone, I said goodbye, and she mumbled "I love you, Mil."

The next morning I went to my office, and was telling my colleagues that she was getting better. Then I was called back to the hospital stat. Ruth Ann cancelled my appointments for the next week or so and did some necessary trouble-shooting for me. When I got to the hospital I found Jessie, Glynne and her husband Kris, and Paula and Lorna together with Dr. Rabinowitz. She told me that Lou had been found in the early morning to have very low blood pressure. Action was immediately taken, she went back to the OR and Dr. Penn found her liver had burst. She was hemorrhaging intra-abdominally, and the surgeon did his best to pack her to stop the bleeding. She went to the ICU, where she had very good nursing care, but never regained consciousness. After four days my neurologist friend, Dr. Marvin Goldstein, came in to examine her, doing several tests. He said she was clearly dead, but Glynne's husband wanted to have a brain wave done to be certain. It was done, and it was totally flat. We gathered around her bed. Glynne talked about some very good memories she had about her mother. There were tears all around. I cried, and Marvin, who was standing behind me, said, "I'm sorry, Millie." I later wrote a note of thanks to him. Lynn flew in immediately from Fargo.

Lou's memorial service was held at First Church of Christ in Parma where Jess and Glynne had grown up and where Jessie was now quite active. However in the last several years, at my church, Lou had participated in several activities, especially the Artists' Group, and everyone agreed to ask my minister, Dick Gilbert, to co-officiate. Jessie, Glynne, and I decorated the funeral parlor with dozens of items she created, paintings and clothes. It was a beautiful service. A great number of my friends came, and Trudy commented to me that that was a tribute to me. Lorna sat with me. Lou had been my Significant Other for sixteen years. I grieved. During visiting hours, her dentist wept. Jessie, Glynne, and I divided the paintings that were left. Jessie and Glynne are to get mine when I die.

$$\bullet \quad \bullet \quad \bullet$$

Living Alone: Lou had retired at sixty, in 1987, with a grand dinner. We had both looked forward to my retirement and talked about buying a larger motor home and traveling the United States. I had to revise my plans. I decided to retire June 30, 1998, at age seventy and a half. That was a critical number in the retirement systems. I applied for both Medicare and Social Security at their appropriate times and also got long-term care insurance.

I needed a new doctor, as the one I had been seeing for rare visits, Dr. Ronald Penna, took himself out on disability because of a neck problem. I wasn't comfortable with any others in his office, so I asked Dr. Rabinowitz to refer me to an internist in her practice: Dr. Bernard Sussman. I liked him right away. It was just in the nick of time because I was beginning to have old age illnesses. The first to be treated was my osteoarthritis, in my ankles, upper back and neck, and knuckles. He put me on one of the new anti-inflammatories. Next was my stomach. I was having more and more heartburn, with reflux. He put me on an antacid.

A few months after Lou's death, the Greece Arts Group held a small exhibit in her memory, raffling off one of her paintings. Paula and her two children were there. I stood leaning against a post, holding the infant Sary in my arms. Suddenly I lost my balance and fell to my left onto concrete and pebbles. I had the presence of mind as I fell to lift Sary upward to my right, so no part of her struck the ground. This was the first of numerous falls I had which later had to be investigated.

Some time in these months I was visiting Paula and her family for dinner. A friend, Nancy Martinez, was also there. My knee began paining me, so I could barely walk. I think it was my left knee. As I got ready to leave, Nancy took my arm and helped me walk. My car was way in the back, so it was a long painful, very slow walk. As we started up the driveway, Paula came out and said, "You're not going home!" I stayed overnight. The next day, it was still excruciating. One of them took me to a medical supply store, and I bought a pair of crutches. The following several days I went to work with crutches and came in the back door, which was on the second floor where my office was. The other colleagues helped me by putting a note downstairs for my patients to come up at their appointment times. In a couple of days my knee was getting better, and after a few days I could discard the crutches. I kept them for future reference. I know all about using crutches! I kept them in the trunk of my car.

My weight was still a problem, and I realized that I badly needed to exercise. Lou owned an exercycle, and from time to time I had used it regularly. In January 1997, I joined the Northwest YMCA, not far from home, and started using the fitness machines according to instructions. I used them twice a week and was consistent in it until I moved, but didn't lose any weight!

After Lou's death, the house felt very empty. I carried on my usual activities and work, but realized I really needed a pet with me, and I chose a cat. I learned about Korats, which have only the outer coat of fur and are supposed, on that account, to be less allergenic. Both Lynn and Lorna are allergic to cats, and I learned later so were Lorna's mother and sister Pinti.

I checked the Internet and found that there are very few Korat breeders. The closest one was in New Hampshire. I contacted them. They had a seven-month-old female, and I arranged to drive there and get it.

The meeting with the breeder couple and their two cats, mother and daughter, was very pleasant. They put the baby kitten in my lap, and she immediately jumped out. That should have been a warning to me. We did the paperwork, finalized the contract, and talked about her care. They carried the cat to my car and put her in the carrier. I stayed that night in a motel. After taking the carrier to my room, I let her out. I should have shut her in the bathroom. The next morning I had to get her out from under the bed. I had a terrible time. I even brought in one of the crutches from the car, but had no luck. I finally got hold of her tail and pulled. She wouldn't let me get near her otherwise. It was Labor Day 1997. I named her Argie, for Grey Purrls (pedigree name) Argentum (Latin for silver).

Argie

Wally, Paula, me, Lynne — Paula's graduation

When we did get home, I shut her in my bathroom. I would try frequently to pet her; she kept hiding behind the fixtures, and if I reached for her she would hiss at me. From my bedroom, being right next to the bathroom, I could easily hear her. The first two nights she cried all night, I think missing her mother, who had been her only companion. I felt very sorrowful for her. She had been kept in the kitchen with her mother, with minimal interaction with humans, and was extremely shy. Because the breeder put her in the carrier in the car, I wasn't prepared for her extreme shyness and fear. Argie didn't allow me to touch her for a full year. When she was to be spayed and later declawed, a house call veterinarian came and tranquilized her and took her to the hospital. He had a hard job tranquilizing her, twice.

In that first year she had several adventures in addition to the vet. At Christmas time I thought I'd lost her completely, even put flyers in neighborhood mailboxes. *Ten days later*, the day after Christmas, I heard a sound from a closet I thought had not been opened. There she was, on the highest shelf. No food, water, or litter box use for ten days! Another time she got down into the basement where there were endless pipes and obstacles that she could hide behind. I asked for Paula's help, and she found her behind a pipe, but of course Argie immediately ran from that spot. Finally after chasing a while, she got behind the washing machine. Rather than trying directly, I built a fence of boards and cardboard that led to the stairs, and let her be. Eventually she did come upstairs. Another time Jess and Glynne were both there and determined to catch her. Jess cornered her in a room. Glynne crouched at the doorway intent on catching her as she ran from Jessie. She ran all right, so fast she just leaped over Glynne, landing first on Glynne's back and producing some severe scratches. This was before she was declawed. We made no more attempts to catch her. When anyone wanted to, I dissuaded them. I talked a lot to her and reached toward her a lot, trying to gain her confidence. She did find and kill two mice.

A year after I got her, I went away for ten days to see Lynn in Fargo while friends fed Argie (without ever even having seen her except through the front window where she liked to perch). While in Fargo, I fell getting out of the shower, breaking three ribs. On my return, Argie followed me and yelled for three hours and began to warm up, first playing with my fingers while I stood behind a chair so she couldn't see me or my connection to the fingers. Progress continued. Three months later she began to curl into a ball at my feet, when I was seated, and one day I boldly reached down and picked her up into my lap! And she let me! And I heard her purr for the first time. From then on we got closer and closer. Now she sleeps with me and frequently comes to my lap or sits behind me in my chair. We have a wonderful bond. This had been another decade of many changes in my life.

Mildred — age 70

Retirement

A year before my planned retirement in July 1998, I started to tell my patients, first the longest-term patients. This is standard practice so they can work through the necessary adjustment and even do some of the grieving in advance so they will be ready to leave. This worked well for most of my patients. Part of the process is the giving back. It was very gratifying to receive gifts, not of great financial value, but meaningful to both me and my patient. Some of these were artistic works by the patients. These are precious to me and they are on display where I live.

Two of my patients, however, ran into trouble in this process. One was a very long-term patient that I had been seeing since my early RPC days, the same one whose record was examined by the State Health Department. She had bad arthritis of both knees and decided during that year to get knee replacement surgeries. She wanted to have this done while I could still be supportive to her. As a consequence, there was a much-reduced time for "working through" the necessary loss. Fortunately I was able to transfer her to a fine psychiatrist-therapist who helped her do a "post working-through."

The second patient was a young woman who talked so continuously in her sessions, that I had to work hard to say anything, therapeutic or otherwise. In our very last session I discovered that I had never announced my retirement to her! This was horrifying to me, and after apologizing greatly to her, I tried to transfer her to a fine therapist, Mary Young, whom I knew from Western Monroe, now being in an office nearer where my patient lived. My patient tried to act accepting of the problem, but I was sure she would have a serious grief reaction. I hope my transferal efforts worked out, but I wasn't able to verify this before leaving. Remembering these two cases keeps me humble. There have been other cases occasionally where I was less totally effective than I should have been, that add to my humility.

So I couldn't feel entirely free. I lost a lot of good relationships too, and I had to work through all this with my therapist, Ray Babineau. I continued to see him weekly.

A few weeks before the retirement, Paula, Lorna, and the two children were visiting Lorna's sister Pinti in Salamanca, Spain. They were called back home early, because their third child, a little boy, was ready to be adopted. They got him at four days of age, in Philadelphia. His name is Etienne Jamal Jaylon. He made us laugh a lot. His hair was kinky from birth.

My Beth friends, Struever and Jelsma, arranged a lovely retirement dinner and festivities at a large restaurant in June 1998. I was gratified by the number of friends from different parts of my life who came. I received a number of gifts. Paula, among others, spoke. Others had mentioned how they got to know me. Paula was the only one who "knew me from birth!" I love to remember that occasion.

After retirement, I no longer needed to wear dress shoes, even for church; the choir didn't sing in the summer. The ones I had were very old, so I took to wearing sneakers all the time, especially after my move, until I discovered the Fash'n Fit store in East Brunswick (see next chapter, also "My So-Called Handicap").

Paula and Lorna, in 1998, had to move to a larger house to accommodate the growing family. They found a lovely one on East Avenue, in a very different type of neighborhood. They had purposely lived in a mixed neighborhood before and made many neighbor friends. They truly believed in diversity. East Avenue was more "upper class," with wider spread of neighbors. The house had a very large backyard, with a pool. Plans were to renovate one side of the house into an apartment for me. I went in the pool a few times, but found I could no longer float or swim. I went under water at the deep end and felt disoriented as to which way was up or down. I panicked until Paula and Lorna pulled me out. I've wondered if that disorientation was a forewarning of the Parkinson's.

On December 31, 1998, I was arriving at their house to celebrate New Year's Eve. As the door was opened, Sary came and hugged me and gave me a very little push. I fell backward and hit my neck/head on a corner of concrete. Lorna asked Paula to call 911, while she (Lorna) held my head at a flat level. It was very cold and snowy, and she crouched at my head holding it. She got very tired and cold. Finally she substituted some clothes under my head. The ambulance came, put me on a board (the fear was, could I have fractured my neck?), and the medic talked small talk to keep me conscious. Lorna followed in her car. In the Strong E.D. I was examined and a CAT scan done. There were no fractures or compressions, thank goodness. I returned to their house with Lorna and, late, we ate New Year's Eve dinner.

This was my third major fall. There had been some smaller ones. Once in New York City I tried to run across a street and fell before on-coming traffic. I barely made it to the curb. At some point I realized I *couldn't run.* I needed to consult my internist. He found my balance indeed bad, and referred me to a widely respected neurologist, Dr. Mike Dunn, who was in Dr. Marvin Goldstein's office! I saw Marvin while waiting for Dr. Dunn, and he commented that he had seen "it" (Parkinson's) coming by my gait when he saw me at the SCMR concerts. (His and his wife's seats were directly in front of Lou's and mine.) Dr. Dunn asked for a CAT scan of my neck because there is a neck condition that could cause the same symptoms. It was normal. Dr. Dunn's diagnosis, when other signs were noted also, was early Parkinson's disease, which had been hinted at by Marvin. For some reason I wasn't floored by this, in spite of the fact that a male friend of mine at church was undergoing a very rapid decline from this awful disease. He certainly had a different form than I did, mine progressing so much more slowly. I saw Dr. Dunn every six months. No medicines were needed yet, but I learned to be more cautious about my posture, turning, and carrying things in front of me. At church one day I was bringing in a box of books and fell forward on the books. There was quite a commotion, as the lobby was full of people.

My cousin Ted, the oldest of Aunt Gladys' four children, suddenly (to me) came to Rochester to be hospitalized at Genesee Hospital because his lung cancer was recurring seriously. I visited him there, and we had a nice conversation. However, the new treatments they used did not help a lot, and later in 1999 he died at his home in Norwich, New York. He was eighty-four. I, with Paula and Lynn, sent flowers to his funeral.

Lorna during the next year realized she was going to have to leave her job, due to her chairman's discrimination against her. Also Paula was disenchanted with Geneseo, with larger classes, and more impersonality among colleagues and with students than there had been at Hamilton. Lorna was even beginning job-hunting at the time of their move to the larger house. They did not tell me this, and I wondered why they didn't start any of their planned renovations of the house they now lived in.

Around Christmas time 1999, Paula explained all this to me. At that time, Lorna had a fairly firm job offer in New Brunswick, New Jersey. I was flabbergasted. They were inviting me to move with them and live with them. This would mean leaving Rochester and so many friends and activities that I loved so much. It took a little while to make this decision. The one idea I had that would make it easier was that I would return to Rochester every few months for a week's visit. At first I thought I could do this monthly, but later it became a plan of every two to three months.

Lorna's parents would also move, and also Dr. Darlene Gibbon, Lorna's professional colleague in gynecology-oncology.

Christmas 1999 had one unfortunate incident. Wilma, Paula's nanny, and her husband Dave, who came as Santa Claus, visited on Christmas Eve.

Eric and Lynn

They brought with them a lovely gift for Paula and Lorna. It was a large glass ball with a Christmas scene and falling snow. Mistakenly, Paula allowed Saraiah to carry it around. Of course it dropped and broke. Sary was quite distressed, and I took her aside while Paula very carefully swept up the glass and debris.

I think Paula didn't say enough to Wilma about it. Wilma was of course distressed, and over the next several weeks got depressed and started missing work. This had a very bad effect on Paula, who was still commuting daily to Geneseo. Paula became furious at Wilma and terminated her by phone. We did not see Wilma again. Surprisingly to me, the children never asked for her. I was very unhappy about these events and wish it could have been handled differently; if, for example, I had talked with Wilma.

In January 2000, I flew to Fargo for Lynn's marriage to Eric. January in Fargo is not a drawing card. So it was a small wedding (Wally didn't come, but Paula did). It was lovely, however, with a very nice reception at a small party house across the Red River in Minnesota. Lynn gave all their female family lovely vases, engraved with Lynn and Eric's names and the date. I got to meet Miriam Garber, Eric's mother, and we made a nice connection. Her husband had died several months before. I stayed at Lynn's and Eric's house for a couple of days. Eric has diabetes, which he cares for minimally.

Argie was very glad to see me on my return and was none the worse for loneliness.

During the next several months, Lorna made many trips back and forth to establish the parameters of the new job. She was to be the new Director of Gynecological Oncology at the recently built Cancer Institute of New Jersey, associated with Robert Wood Johnson Medical Center and Rutgers University. Lorna was in fact planning and building her own department. It was a wonderful opportunity.

Paula, Lorna, and the three children and a couple of times I, went to New Brunswick and stayed a few days at a hotel, in order to house-hunt. After one false start (they chose a beautiful house, but it turned out to be too close to a toxic dump), we found what we wanted in East Brunswick, with many favorable aspects. It had a two-room extension that could, with quite a lot of renovation, be made into an apartment. By this time I had come to terms with the idea of moving, as long as I could make the return trips, and began to pack.

Much of my furniture, clothes, and books, to go from an eight-room house to a two-room apartment, had to be given away in one way or another. Lou's daughters took a lot, especially Jessie. I gave away medical books to a Russian medical group; and a lot of clothes and accessories to the YWCA and Salvation Army. I gave all my thirty-three-rpm records to WXXI for auction. That was hard—the collection included some very fine recordings that I never had even listened to. Looking back, I'm amazed I was able to organize and accomplish all this in a timely way. I did have some help. A choir friend, Grace Carswell, spent a day with me doing some difficult letter sorting; and Jess was a tremendous help.

The United States was still having a financial boom (but it ended soon after) and I felt comfortable with my assets. I decided to give a legacy gift to The Nature Conservancy (TNC), my favorite charity. To me, our most crucial concern in this world, is what we are doing to the environment, our planet and its resources. This legacy would actually give me a small annuity. In the process of doing this, I was visited by a TNC official. We talked a while. I felt benevolent and friendly, and after a while, Argie actually came to him and sniffed his fingers!

In 2000, a month before my moving, I bought a new-to-me second-hand computer from my consultant Steve Gern. It is a Power Macintosh G3, with OS 8.6. It has more memory and is able to incorporate more upgrades than the Performa, and so far it has done well. I gave the Performa to my grandchildren. It still has some patient data on its hard drive, so I don't want it to go outside the family nor to an adult that could search it. I use the new one for documents, letters, a lot of e-mail, playing Solitaire and Scrabble, and occasional Web searches. And now this autobiography.

Also in June 2000, my Barnard College class celebrated our fiftieth anniversary at our class reunion. We were indeed a special class. We had brought in the largest amount ever for the Alumnae Fund that year! We were told we were role models for all other classes. The class reunion was fun. We had a number of small gatherings, plus a grand dinner at the renovated top floor of the graduate women's residence. I met with Gladys Lerner, my only co-major in physics. She had made a tremendous effort to get to the reunion, as she was and had been very ill for a long time with kidney disease, had had one transplant and was on dialysis again. She looked terrible, with a gray skin, but it was wonderful to see her. She died a few months later.

One of my best friends in our class, who had also been in the Chapel Choir, was Sally Salinger Lindsay. She had come to the first several choir reunions, but died a number of years ago from a slow-growing osteosarcoma.

Both Paula and Lorna and I put our houses on the market. The process went smoothly. Paula's house ultimately went to a prominent Rochester politician. My house went to a couple that was very enthusiastic about it. Lorna's parents had been renting so they didn't have to go through this.

The week that Paula left Rochester, with me still there, was very eventful for me. On the previous Monday, at a regular physical from my internist, he found a breast lump. I had a mammogram on Thursday, and when I mentioned it to the radiologist, she did a needle biopsy. I was impressed with her attitude and skill. She called me on Monday, after Paula had gone, and let me know, with apologies and regret, that the biopsy was a carcinoma. I was not surprised; all my adult life I had expected it.

That week I did last-minute things and got Argie's things ready. Paula's family and Lorna's parents moved in a caravan of four moving trucks on July 21, 2000. Lorna's parents "belonged" to one of the trucks; they had bought a house in North Brunswick, a few minutes away from E.B. My move was one week later, but my moving company messed up on dates and had to put my things in storage for a week. Argie and I drove to our new home in East Brunswick on July 28, and Paula and three children welcomed me beautifully. For the next week, they helped me survive without my belongings and my stuff came one week later. I weighed 172! Argie was still very wary with anyone but myself.

I thought a lot about my career and retirement. I felt I had given all I could to the patients who came to me, with a few exceptions, and likewise the therapists and others that I supervised and taught. I had few (referring back to some cases I didn't do well with) regrets about the service I'd rendered. Aside from psychotherapy, I had used "chemotherapy" (my high school wish) in my work to its fullest. About my marriage, I had many regrets and disappointments. Wally's a good man basically, but I couldn't live comfortably with him. Lou and I had some difficulties, but mostly we clicked splendidly. My daughters were well on their ways to very good lives. Retirement was treating me well.

Full Circle, Back to New Jersey

Upon my arriving and being beautifully welcomed in East Brunswick in July 2000, there were four things I had to attend to: the apartment renovations; my furniture; my driver's license; and the cancer. Regarding the first, bars and rails had already been put in the bathroom and on my outdoor steps. A handyman, Ed, was beginning to work on the rest, making two separated rooms into two connected rooms. Argie was confined to the bathroom until my back door leading to Paula's living room was complete. My furniture arrived before this was completed, so the movers had to bring things into either room through two different doors. Renovations included the installing of glass doors on my two openings into the house proper so Argie could be kept from the house. (We had found that Argie was not hypoallergenic, unfortunately.) Next, a doorway had to be made in the wall between my bedroom (which had been built as a maid's room) and the sitting room.

After that was done, Argie and I had two rooms, connected together, but separated from the rest of the house. Argie, who had been kept in the bathroom until the back glass door was in, enjoyed exploring the new room. My sitting room has a cathedral ceiling, with a consequent empty space on the high wall. I had Lou's paintings hung there, as if it were a gallery. In my bedroom, I also had shelves put high up around four walls (as Lou had in our kitchen), and on them placed my pretty things, most of which were gifts from patients and family. They included my Hummel figures, many vases, figurines, bird figures, animal figures, an elephant bell my cousin George (Ledget) brought back from his military service in India, and my valedictory trophy.

The next thing to attend to, really in the midst of the renovations as that progressed slowly, was the cancer. Lorna, Paula's gynecologist partner, connected me to a breast surgeon, Dr. McManus. She immediately stopped my hormone replacement, which I'd taken for fifteen years or so. Dr. McManus found on my recent x-rays from Rochester, a different cancer in each breast, lobular in the left and DCIS (ductal carcinoma in situ) in the right, and in August she did two lumpectomies. These were done on an ambulatory basis, so there was very little down time. Paula was my ride and my moral support. There was minimal pain associated. The two biopsies were as predicted, but the DCIS needed a more definitive removal and further treatment. I was referred to an oncologist, Dr. Toppmeyer, at the Cancer Institute. She said my choices were a right mastectomy, or another lumpectomy followed by radiation. In either case, an auxiliary "sentinel" node would also be taken to check for metastases. Dr. Toppmeyer recommended the latter. So in September that's what I had done: a second lumpectomy and a node removal, both on the right. The node came back negative, so all I needed was radiation on the breast and no chemotherapy. Paula accompanied me for all these appointments and again the surgery was ambulatory.

About the driver's license—I wish I'd known that I could drive my New York car indefinitely as a guest in New Jersey. To get a New Jersey license I had to have it completed in sixty days. It was a horror of times, documents, rudeness, and inefficiency at the Motor Vehicle Agency. On my first visit, not only was the initial line long, but after my first encounter I sat and waited five hours because the clerk didn't put my papers in the right place. I finally asked. Then I needed another document. All told, I had to make five visits, each with a long wait or waits, on five different days, requiring new documents each time. They didn't tell me at the beginning all that would be needed. Finally, about one week before the sixty days were up, I was told about the requirement of a certified copy of my divorce to show I'm still the same person as the name on my birth certificate! I sent a certified letter to the (Rochester) Monroe County Clerk and sent a return stamped certified envelope. Thankfully they heeded my need, and I received the document on the fifty-ninth day! Over the next months and years there was a lot in the news about scandals and inefficiency of the New Jersey Motor Vehicle Agency.

In October I took my first trip back to Rochester. I had originally planned to do it in September, but the cancer ruled that out. I went by train. Paula took me to the New Brunswick station and this time accompanied me to Penn Station, New York City. I got to know the vagaries of NJ Transit and Amtrak. In Rochester I had dinner with my WI group, sang in the choir, and had meals with other friends. I stayed for three days with Caroll Revak, and then with Kas and Larry Eldridge from the choir. Unfortunately, I scraped their car in backing out of their driveway in the dark. I paid for repairs. The week was very happy and I came home refreshed. I have done this every three or four months since, staying with different friends each time, except that I have stayed with Glynne several times.

At home in October 2000, I had to get measured and tatooed (marked up) for the radiation treatments. During one of the first preparatory sessions, the technician left the room for a while, leaving my chest uncovered. The room was multi-purpose, also a library, and while I lay there uncovered, someone walked in to use the library. I complained to the social worker, and she evidently took it up at a staff meeting. (Finally I was less submissive!) I'm not sure why it took so long, but the treatments finally began in early December and were daily (weekdays) until January 28. There were no problems, burns or anything, and I felt fine except for slight fatigue. Follow-up mammograms have always been clear. On my follow-up with Dr. Toppmeyer, she prescribed Tamoxifen and a few months later, Megace, a progesterone product, to counteract the hot flashes I was getting from the Tamoxifen.

I believe I'm also at high risk for ovarian cancer, as an aunt (Auntie Nan) and a paternal cousin (Louise) died of it. So I'm getting exams and ultrasounds every six months. My gynecologist for this is Dr. Darlene Gibbon, Lorna's professional partner, who moved here from Rochester with the rest of us.

I injured my right knee by sharply bending it and tearing a cartilage. It was very painful. I saw an orthopedist, who told me it could be operated on but it would probably slowly get better anyway, which it *very* slowly did. Then I fell on the garage floor, hitting the same knee. Although it eventually recovered pretty much, I still get occasional twinges in it and in climbing stairs it is definitely weaker than my left, but still improving.

At Christmastime 2000 I got a call from Martin! He was my med school boyfriend and has lived for years in Seattle, Washington. He was now visiting his daughter and her spouse in New York City, as they were shortly to move to Texas. He came out to East Brunswick on Christmas Eve Day to visit me and have dinner with my family. His train ride was very problematical. They had to stop and wait three hours in the middle of nowhere. We were lucky that we now all had cell phones. I finally met him at the New Brunswick station. What a joyful reunion! He got acquainted with Paula and her family. The children put on an after-dinner show for us, which they often do for guests. We had a delightful time. Martin took the train back to New York.

Since moving I have seen more of the Webbs and my cousin Bill, who now lives in a retirement community. I've gone to his place in Maplewood, and we have driven together to visit the Webbs for holidays. Once Betsy, who lives in Pennsylvania, and Fran and Dave and I had lunch with him at his community dining room. It was a very pleasant reunion. We plan to do it again. The Webbs and Bill have also visited us at Christmas, and my sister Fran came by shortly after the move because of my cancer. One time I had a lovely lunch visit with three old friends, Kris, and Steve O., and Fran A. from the Columbia Choir, traveling north from Florida.

I asked a lot of Paula to help me set up my computer and apartment. Finally she got fed up because she was so busy and asked me not to interrupt her during the day, but to make my requests only at breakfast time. I've missed being able to talk with her. In January 2001, I started checking out activities and services in East Brunswick. I already had a good idea of the roads of the New Brunswick area because of so many drives to the hospitals. I found a shoe store, Fash'n Fit, that fitted me with orthopedic shoes from off the shelf. The ones I got had been made for that store by Miner in Batavia near Rochester! I had known about Miner but never tried them out, preferring to have the shoes custom-made so I could have them dressy.

I went to the Unitarian Society of New Brunswick (actually in East Brunswick) and felt well welcomed. Prior to the move I had contacted the church by e-mail and found out they have no choir, but have a relationship with a choral society. I auditioned for it but didn't like the director's methods. There are other choruses around that I will check out.

I immediately joined a Shakespeare reading group at the church, and soon after, their "Visitation Ministry," visiting and helping sick or home-bound members. I also looked at the local Senior Center, which had some activities I became interested in, the first being a cheap lunch and a discussion group, then regular massages, Tai Chi, and podiatric visits. I got one haircut but wasn't satisfied with it. More recently they've offered conversational Spanish. I've been on a couple of all-day field trips to party houses/dinner theatres.

A new YMCA in South Brunswick had just opened, and it includes fitness machines as the Rochester one I had belonged to does. East Brunswick doesn't have one fully outfitted, but will have in two years. I joined the South Brunswick YMCA and have worked out there twice a week. When I moved to East Brunswick, my weight had ballooned to 172. After a year of working out and some dietary reduction, I got down to 162 and have held it since.

I also found the local library, went to some book discussions and foreign films, and have borrowed books and made copies there. I've made friends at both USNB and the Senior Center with whom I've attended concerts, plays (some in New York, some at the Papermill Playhouse), musicals, and dance shows: including Greek and Shakespeare plays.

In May 2001, Paula and Lorna received word that their fourth child, a little girl, was in Philadelphia awaiting adoption. (Paula and Lorna had promised that four would be the end!) This time they had her stay in foster care until they got the result of an HIV test. This was about six weeks, and they and their three older children went to get her. They had in fact been on a vacation trip in Pennsylvania, arrived home, turned around, and went back. This baby is named Noemi' Eillim (Millie backwards). She has a huge crown of kinky hair. Paula has spent many hours learning to braid it in sections, making corn rows and attaching beads. Noemi' still doesn't like this process, but I recall that at that age and also when older Saraiah had very much disliked having her hair done. Noemi' "talks" continuously, gesturing as if carrying on a conversation, and also makes us laugh a lot.

In July 2001, Jessie, Lou's older daughter, was getting remarried in Rochester, to Larry Vacarelli. It was an ideal match. She asked me to be "the mother of the bride" in Lou's stead. She helped me buy a lovely formal pants suit. We had the hems tailored accurately, but when I wore it, the right leg was too short. The tailor must have thought he had made a mistake, and made them equal instead of using his own measurements. It was not a big deal. I did not mention it to Jess or anyone. The wedding was in the same Parma church as Lou's memorial service had been, and was thoroughly lovely. I felt very honored.

The day of the attacks of 9/11, I watched TV all day, a mistake. I spoke to Paula in the morning, but was alone all day when I really needed to talk to someone. The shock made me feel depersonalized. I should have called a friend or Frances. Lorna, in the afternoon, had her parents come here, and we had an outdoor dinner on the deck. Paula didn't like my withdrawal and called me on it. A few weeks later, she and I had a heated discussion of tensions between us, mostly about both of us distancing from each other and mixed expectations. We've both tried to do better, and currently we are doing so.

After 9/11, as so many people did, I began to rethink old relationships. I had thought of Mary J., my best friend from college, many times in the intervening years, but now began to want recontact. I found her quickly, as she was still in Washington, D.C., having retired from the CIA, and though married, had kept her maiden name. She was surprised to hear from me. We hope to see each other, especially as Lynn and Eric will be living in the area.

In 2002 I learned about RU-ALL (Rutgers University-Academy of Lifelong Learning) and started taking ten-session courses. I first took Greek Tragedy. The lecturer was a Rutgers professor, but his delivery was problematic. He never finished a sentence, but kept starting new ones. It was hard to keep track of his points. Since then however I've seen two Greek tragedies on Broadway, which helped my understanding. I've seen, at RU-ALL, three series of different categories of movies. In the fall sessions, I started this autobiography.

My return visits to Rochester have been gratifying. Once I was reading too intently in Penn Station, New York, waiting for the Amtrak announcement, and missed the train! I had to change my ticket to a two-hour later train and missed the choir rehearsal that evening. I've stayed with different friends each time, but several times with Lou's daughter Glynne and her family. Not only have I seen many friends, but also my doctors, though I've gradually switched doctors.

In March 2002, Dr. Dunn started me on an anti-Parkinson drug, which has definitely helped my balance and awkwardness in getting in and out of chairs and cars. I do have a slight, inconsistent tremor which is worse when I'm anxious. Occasionally I still fall; once face down, down my outdoor steps carrying in front of me (a bad position) a heavy bag of old cat litter, but luckily I was not hurt other than bruising. I have a new neurologist, who like previous doctors has advised me to use a cane, especially in the house. I've tried at times, but it is really inconvenient because I'm frequently using both hands for something.

I got a phone call from Martin, surprisingly, suggesting that I plan to come to Seattle to attend the annual Orcas Island Chamber Music Festival on Orcas Island, (in Washington State) where his family has summer homes. The Festival was founded four to five years ago by his daughter Aloysia and is now managed by her. He had suggested this by mail a year or so before. This time I thought seriously about it, thinking I could stop en route to see Eric and Lynn. Martin sent me literature, and I looked into flights and so forth and decided to go.

The plan was to go to Fargo the third week in August and on to Seattle the final week, rent a car and drive, including car ferry, to Orcas, and stay at a resort place (cabins) not far from Martin's house. He, of course, and his wife Laila would be very busy with the festival.

Just before leaving East Brunswick, I heard from Lynn that both she and Eric were looking for jobs back east. Both were suffering unpleasant changes in their job Chairmen. Eric would be away on a job interview so I wouldn't see him, and right after I would leave, both Lynn and Eric would be going to Connecticut for job interviews. My visit with Lynn was fine. She was able to take some time from work for us to do things together. The day before we both left (at almost the same times for our flights), we took the two dogs to a friend's house.

My trip to Seattle was uneventful, except for too long a walk with my luggage to get the car. I drove to Anacortes, took the ferry to Orcas, and drove directly to the concert place just in time for the first concert! I met Aloysia, her spouse Jackie, and Laila, Martin's wife, after the concert and finally found Martin. I stayed six days, enjoyed my cabin, and Martin managed to spend an hour or two with me each day (I hadn't expected him to). He showed me the island which is beautiful and mountainous, had me to breakfast with him and Laila once, and invited me to a rehearsal that included him one morning. I also met Sophie, Aloysia's and Jackie's daughter, three years old. She's talkative, in constant motion, and delightful.

I enjoyed two concerts, but because of the ferry and plane scheduling, had to miss the third and last. To meet the only ferry that would get me to the airport on time, I had to take an evening one, then drive all night back to Seattle and then to wait two hours at the airport. Even on the plane though, I did not sleep. Paula and Lorna picked me up at Newark. It was a wonderful trip, and seeing Martin was such a joy! The concerts were a real pleasure.

Lynn and Eric ultimately got jobs, Eric in Silver Springs, Maryland, and Lynn at the University of Connecticut. So they had to resume their long-distance relationship, driving or flying back and forth on weekends. The dogs went back and forth too, staying with one and then the other. Now Lynn has an offer as an administrator at NIH, but it will take a few months to tie all the loose strings. She and Eric are buying a house, and Lynn will move down in August.

My new internist thought my stomach problem was bad enough to warrant an endoscopy. Another ambulatory procedure. It revealed a large hiatus hernia, but no Barrett's epithelium (which portends throat cancer). With medicine I keep the heartburn under good control.

Paula has taken up self-defense (Hrav Maga, an Israeli type). She's instructing at the karate school several nights a week, and the three older children are taking karate there. She goes to annual weeklong workshops for training. She had decided that she wouldn't teach college again. Lorna's job takes more and more of her time, usually working well into evenings.

During my most recent visit to Rochester, in February, 2003, I saw many friends but had one horrendous experience. I was driving north to a friend's house in Webster and was only in Fairport when I thought I had arrived. I couldn't find the right house, so parked the car to look on foot. The first house I chose required me to walk across a lawn with two feet of snow and then climb over a snow bank into their drive. Just before getting to the snow bank, I fell forward, but was able to get up. Then I fell backwards, and couldn't get up. It was getting dark and I was not very visible. I struggled every way I could think of to get up, resting every little while. I think I lay in the snow for a good forty-five minutes. Finally I was able to kick some snow off the snow bank, and I slid down to the drive. The woman at that house told me her house number, but had no interest in helping me. I then walked down the sidewalk to check other houses. I was covered, of course, with snow. A young woman drove up near me and asked if I was in trouble. I said "Yes," and she invited me into her car. I was soaked and exhausted. Her name is Jeanne Budgeon. She helped me figure out where I had gone wrong, called my friend (by then I was an hour late), and nurtured me for a little while, drove me to where my car was parked, and set me on my way. When I got to my friend Joyce's house, she gave me some clothes to wear and put mine in the dryer. The visit was fine. I sent Jeanne some flowers the next day, and she wrote me a lovely note. I shall never forget her thoughtful kindness, and luckily because of her my ordeal ended happily.

I celebrated my seventy-fifth birthday while in Rochester and was given three different parties!

The Rochester Unitarian Church is in turmoil. Dick Gilbert and his wife retired in June 2002. The new Interim Minister has been controversial. And the Religious Education Minister has been terminated by the Executive Board, and I have many misgivings about the process they used. I feel ready to become a member of the USNB here. I've got roots here now, but will continue going to Rochester to sing and see friends. I signed the Membership Book of USNB on April 6, 2003, at about the same time that the Society's name was changed to "The Unitarian Society, a Unitarian Universalist Congregation." Now I'm part of it.

Appendix I
Wally's History

Wally grew up in Erie, PA. He was the oldest of three, with six years between each pair. He was very brilliant in school. After graduation, he was a navy medic for two years at the Great Lakes Naval Hospital and learned a little bit of medicine. After that, he used the GI Bill of Rights to attend and graduate from Gannon College in Erie. Otherwise he might not have gone to college; he was the first in his family. He worked summers at International Paper Co. in Erie.

He moved to Rochester for an engineering job at Kodak. He began to listen to and enjoy classical music, and got into recording a lot for friends and others. He took up the accordion, and much later, as our family grew, bought himself a wonderful electronic organ, which he learned to play. He got an early computer when they first came out, and became an expert at using it.

He retired shortly after I left him. He keeps himself very busy with his hobbies. He remarried in 1984, but his wife died tragically after five years.

INDEX